Not Every Sea Hath Pearls

by

Loulie Albee Mathews

A Prism Edition

Naturegraph Publishers, Inc.

ISBN 0-87961-164-2   cloth
ISBN 0-87961-165-0   paper

"O Brother! Not every sea hath pearls; not every branch will flower, nor will the nightingale sing thereon. Then, ere the nightingale of the mystic paradise repair to the garden of God, and the rays of the heavenly morning return to the Sun of Truth—make thou an effort, . . . "

The Seven Valleys, Bahá'u'lláh

Dedicated
To the Latin American Pioneers
and
The Latin American Bahá'ís

CONTENTS

Part Four
THE INVISIBLE WORLD

Part Five
ACROSS THE SEVEN SEAS

Part Six
SOUTH AFRICA

CONCLUSION

PREFACE

As time propells us further from the heroic age of the Bahá'í Faith and its early formative days, accounts such as this increase in their value to inspire and inform us of the spiritual grandeur of those early God-intoxicated lovers who carried the torch of Faith into the remotest reaches of the globe for their well-beloved 'Abdu'l-Bahá and Shoghi Effendi. These are the words of such a one, called by the Master " 'Abdu'l-Bahá's lion" who would "roar across the Seven Seas." They give us an intimate glimpse of what it meant to be a Bahá'í during those days when only a handful of Bahá'ís were spread across the face of a continent, laboring to erect the rudiments of an administrative order that could only be perceived as the embryo of the future Heavenly Kingdom of God upon earth. But such was their vision, their steadfastness that they strode forward, with joy and humor, in sickness or health, often in the face of intense criticism or personal danger.

This new edition of *Not Every Sea Hath Pearls*, with an introduction by the author's daughter, presents once again the exciting, often humorous, stories of Loulie's Bahá'í life. It is here clarified that the author's memoirs do not constitute sacred scripture, nor the official view of any Bahá'í institution.

Loulie Albee Mathews

INTRODUCTION

Loulie Shaw Albee, my mother, was born in Newcastle, New Hampshire, October 12, 1869. Her father, John Albee, associate professor of Greek at Harvard University, consorted with many eminent men of the time, among whom were Henry and William James; Henry Wadsworth Longfellow, who wrote a poem for his wife; and Alexander Graham Bell. Upon Bell's invention of the telephone, he came to the Albee's home and said, "John, put this piece of metal to your ear and see if you can hear my voice." Mr. Bell then moved into another room, spoke into the other part of the device, and asked John, "Do you hear me?" "Yes," said John Albee, "and so will all the world."

Loulie's mother, Harriet Ryan Albee, was an ardent Catholic, who also studied for the Unitarian ministry. From the age of sixteen Harriet's empathy for the poor, the elderly and the sick emerged. She was known to exchange places with the feeblest of the elderly waiting in line to reach the Boston Soup Kitchens. In bad weather, and after patiently waiting, she would personally deliver the soup to their homes. Frequently, she stood in the queue most of the day. During this time, Harriet learned that many individuals around here were dying of a mysterious disease called consumption, and since the hospitals refused to take them in, they had nowhere to go for help. Harriet appealed to Dr. William Ellery Channing, the rector of a Unitarian Church in Boston, to house these individuals in his vestry.

Thus was born The Channing Home, one of the first hospices in the country, which eventually moved to larger quarters and lasted a hundred years, only closing its doors in 1958. Her dedication to serving the elderly and ailing ended when she herself died of tuberculosis, shortly after giving birth to her daughter, Loulie Shaw Albee.

Then faced with the urgent questions of how to raise and educate a motherless little girl, John Albee decided Loulie should follow her mother's faith. At the age of eight, Loulie was sent to a convent boarding school, where the poor food, constant discipline and lack of laughter made an indelible impression upon her spirit. Once out of the convent, she wanted nothing further to do with organized institutions, particularly religious ones.

In September 1898, Loulie married Edward Roscoe Mathews, a Harvard graduate, whose father presented him with a seat on the New York Stock Exchange as a wedding present. Four years after their move to New York, a daughter, Wanden Esther Mathews, was born.

Loulie didn't miss the ordinary lifestyle of New England, and in fact, thrived on the exciting pulse of New York. Always actively involved with people and interested in just about everything, Loulie boldly rose above the expectations of women in that period and visited prisons with the beautiful lady lawyer, Inez Mulholland, marched up Fifth Avenue in a suffragette parade, and founded a home for working girls. When Loulie's activities became too embarrassing for my father's male pride, he retired to his club.

The United States declared war in April 1917. My mother's fervent desire to be of service more than likely enabled her to obtain a passport, which was considered a near impossibility at that time. With torpedoes sizzling around the ship, she sailed to France, where, for the following six months, she served in a hospital for the burned close behind the French combat lines.

Having drifted away from the Catholic Church, Loulie became fascinated by fortune tellers, mediums and occult phenomena of all sorts. Fortunately, she met Mrs. Asa Neath Cocheran, who taught, among several other things, numerology. During their many visits in

Mrs. Cocheran's home, mother was always drawn to and fascinated by a particular picture. When she finally asked, "Who is that wonderful person?," Mrs. Cocheran initially refused to tell her, encouraging her to finish her lesson. But during the next visit Mrs. Cocheran offered more, "His name is 'Abdu'l-Bahá. He is the son of Bahá'u'lláh, which means 'the Glory of God.' You must never forget his name or his face." Mrs. Cocheran shared some of Bahá'u'lláh's writings with Loulie and told her that when the time was right she would learn more.

Not until the fall of 1917 were Mrs. Cocheran's words fulfilled. Enroute to Boston from our home in Portsmouth, New Hampshire, mother and I were in a car accident and hospitalized. Harry Randal, mother's cousin, came to our rescue and we recovered in his home. A Bahá'í who escorted 'Abdu'l-Bahá to Elliot, Maine, in 1912, to visit the property that is now the Green Acre Bahá'í School, Harry bathed us in the light of the Bahá'í Revelation. Between her initial contact with Mrs. Cocheran and the unexpected visit with Harry, Loulie made up her mind, "There! That's it," she said, and from that moment to the end of her life, she directed all energies to serving the Bahá'í Faith.

I fondly remember a particular journey with my mother. In the fall of 1925 sailing home from Porto Fino on an Italian liner, we noted among the passengers a distinguished dark gentleman. After speculating over what nationality he might be, we invited him to sit with us and asked him. "I am Dr. W. E. B. DuBois and I am an American Negro." Rather embarrassed that we had been missing an entire group of our fellow citizens, mother and I vowed to make efforts to become familiar with the thinking, writing and teachings of the American Negro. It was through Dr. DuBois that we met James Weldon Johnson, an eminent and most charming Negro poet who was hard at work on his book, *God's Trombones.* Countee Cullen and Langston Hughes, younger black poets, we had the privilege of entertaining as well. In addition, Mrs. Mary McCloud Bethune, who raised enough money to start her own school in Georgia, was a guest in our home for a couple of weeks. This visit ended sadly however. My father tried to reserve a drawing room for her on the train returning from New York to Washington, but was told that no parlor car space could be sold to colored people. Despite my father's furious protest, discrimination won out.

Mother was not only charming and pretty, but her incredible enthusiasm entered into her relationships with all people, no matter what race. I think, due to our initial experience with Dr. DuBois, she was especially partial to mingling with the Black race. Even at the age of ninety-two, she taught a dance class to a group of small black children in Florida. Truly, she was a dynamo of energy that never stopped.

In *Not Every Sea Hath Pearls*, my mother not only shares her outward experiences as a Bahá'í but also her tests and difficulties in the conquest for spiritual maturity. 'Abdu'l-Bahá often said that the longest road in the world is from the head to the heart. This book shares the circumstances of an incredible woman along that road.

Mrs. Wanden Kane
August 28, 1983

Part One
The Gift of Faith

Chapter 1

THE PHOTOGRAPH

I sailed on the *Ile de France* the last week of July, 1914. I was weary and longing for a glimpse of the U. S. A. I had no intimation that an era was closing and that war and rumors of war were now to be the fate of the world for many years to come. The sea had the pale blue tint of midsummer and lay flat as a parquet floor. The Captain, with whom I had crossed before, invited me to tea on the bridge. As our eyes swept the horizon they came to rest on a figure hunched over against the steering wheel, misery etched in every line of his body. "Alas," sighed the Captain, "this most excellent sailor sighted a ship that turned out to be a phantom. It was during our last voyage from New York to Havre. No matter how trusted a seaman has been, when that happens he can never again take the helm — that is, never unless war is declared. A phantom ship is an omen of conflict — and there are many records of a full rigged ship emerging from the mist before the coming of war." Four days later we knew that Germany had declared war against France. Our sailor had seen the fatal omen — the ship that foretold death and destruction.

The United States was not yet involved but a great wave of restlessness pervaded the land and I was swept into its vortex. For the first time I realized the instability of my own religious belief and the need of finding the answers to the journey of the soul. The charm of ritual felt in childhood had long since given way to probing the dogmas of the church — those dogmas wrappd in ambiguous terms and so unsatisfactorily explained. In recent years

1

I had investigated two modern movements but their reaction upon me was superficial and had not reached down and clutched my soul. It was at this moment that someone mentioned to me a Mrs. Asa Cocheran who taught a science of numbers and explained the symbolism that one encounters in all religions. I determined to study with her. I found her living opposite Columbia College and hither I went twice a week to take lessons and learn of her mystic interpretations. Our studies were conducted in a small room cluttered with packages of books, papers and letters. My teacher was different from anyone I had known; sometimes she looked old as the Sphinx, with eyes that seemed to hold the secrets of the ages, sometimes she was like a young girl. Her moods reflected a thousand lives. From my first encounter, I felt she possessed a source of power that I could never understand.

One day the colored maid led me into a room I had not known was there; the walls and furniture were painted white and on the table was a single rose, no other ornament. I sat down and looked about; opposite me was a picture, a portrait of a man in oriental dress. He answered my inquiring gaze. The longer I looked into his eyes, the more uncomfortable I became. It was as though I had been standing on a bank and suddenly the solid earth had moved from under my feet. I lost command of myself and was precipitated into a whirlpool. The unreal center which I had built up melted away and I had no support. Engaged as I was in this mental struggle, I did not hear the door open nor did I realize that I was not alone until Mrs. Cocheran sat down beside me. "Who is that man?" I queried. "Never mind who it is, you study your lesson." I bent over the book, but I could not free myself from the sad eyes that had pierced my inner being. I made my way home without knowing that one chapter of my life had closed forever; that I was never to be the same again.

When next I came for a lesson I was shown into the small room with its accustomed disorder. That day Mrs. Cocheran vibrated with life and vigor, age dropped from her shoulders and shadows from her eyes. I hardly recognized her. The moment she saw me she seized my hands and said, "You asked at your last lesson about the picture that hangs in the white room. Well, you shall know, for in your destiny it will play a mighty part. It is a photograph of 'Abdu'l-Bahá, the son of Bahá'u'lláh, the Prophet of God, who has so lately visited this earth. The name "Bahá'u'lláh" means the Glory of God; its vibration is the most powerful on earth. That you may learn of His teachings I am sending you a book on New Year's Eve. It contains the key to that which you seek — read one paragraph before you sleep and do not worry if the meaning is not clear. Hold the words in your mind and presently you will find you do understand them. Bahá'u'lláh alone can alter the current of your life and if you are to fulfill your mission here you must begin to study the Bahá'í Message."

The night of December thirty-first arrived. At this period of my life I had a guardian angel in the person of June, a beautiful Irish girl about my own age, and to her I confided the news of the book that was to arrive at midnight. I related how I had seen the picture in the white room and of the over-powering effect it had had on me. To while away the hours before midnight, June drew from her memory of Ireland stories of the Little People; how on New Year's Eve they would toss up the hay mows, open the barn doors, and even climb the steeples and ring the church bells before the sexton could drive them away. Exactly at five minutes of twelve the front doorbell rang and June went flying over the stairs to answer it. When she pushed open the door of my bedroom she was a different person. Bearing the book above her head she walked as though carrying a torch, her body rigid — her whole expression unearthly as though she had seen a ghost. "Sure, this is something wonderful — this is what you were born for — it is part of your destiny — take hold of it now and never let it go." I unwrapped the book.[1] It was bound in black cloth

[1] This volume is now in the library of the Bahá'í International School at Pine Valley, Colorado.

with "Ighan" in gold lettering — I had not the least idea what the word meant nor how it was pronounced, but I knew I was holding in my hands a treasure and that the treasure was mine! June came and leaned over my shoulder. "There is something written in the front of the book," she said. I had not had time to look at the flyleaf but now saw that the book was inscribed to me as a Bahá'í teacher. Would I ever be that, I wondered — what miracle would be needed to bring about such a transformation? I turned a page at random:

> "Each manifestation of God has a distinct individuality, a definitely prescribed Mission, a predestined Revelation, and specially designated limitations. Each is known by a different Name and is characterized by a special attribute."

Again I opened to another chapter:

> "In whatever age and cycle they are sent down from their invisible habitations of ancient glory into this world, (they come) to educate the souls of men and endow with grace all created things, they are invariably endowed with all-compelling power and invested with invincible sovereignty."

This showed me the first glimpse of the rhythm of the planet. Everything here is recurrent — not only the seasons but civilizations follow one another. There is no single phenomenon — Prophets come and go and come again, following the same law that guides all things here below.

In looking back at this period I believe Mrs. Cocheran planned to teach me herself and what a teacher she was! But, alas! I was not yet emancipated from the standards of the world. I was still bound by limitations of my own generation, so a few weeks later when Mrs. W. K. Vanderbilt invited me to accompany her to Paris I accepted, thinking that such a chance to see the war at first hand was important. This state of mind reminds me of the false emphasis placed on personal appearance by my generation. The casual clothes of today were then unknown. The cult of women of fashion was exclusiveness. Freed from Victorian petticoats and undue modesty we went to town on personality. One's outward appearance must declare that you were not made of common clay — not one of a species but the center of a new creation and to give emphasis to this theory, what you put on had to be unique. Dresses, therefore, were selected from the great establishments of Paris after weeks spent in salons and fitting rooms. A hat could not be bought in a shop — perish the thought! It must be fashioned on the head and be the only one in existence; a trademark of specialness where ere you walked! The high priestess of Felt and Straw in the early days of the century was Reboux and she affixed prices that matched her genius. Louis and Antoine had sprung into being solely to devise hairdos of classic magnificence; each hair was trained — it must accentuate a charm, hide a blemish, or be sheared off. A profile had to attain prestige and we thought nothing of crossing the ocean to visit a noted stylist. The quest of the Golden Fleece was now to find a new neckline! Though the elite traveled far, they remained enclosed within their own citadels and they lowered the porte-cochere only for their intimates, important people, and an occasional troubadour who caught their fancy.

When I came to know Ella Cooper in whose Mother's house the Master had stayed during part of his visit to San Francisco, I asked if 'Abdu'l-Bahá had mentioned how we ought to dress. She reflected a moment and then replied: "Yes. He said, 'We must dress as an example to the rich and a comfort to the poor.'" From that moment I turned my back on fashion and exclusiveness and took a road marked "Universal." "Consort with all the people with love and fragrance. Fellowship is the cause of unity and unity is the source of order in the world," wrote Bahá'u'lláh.

Going to war during those first months was a terrifying experience. From the outset we were plunged into disaster. The crossing of the stormy ocean with its nightly blackout, its black bread and cold — all these discomforts finally culminated with an attack by a submarine that shattered part of the ship's machinery. From then on we were obliged to sleep on deck, life preservers under our heads. Paris, when we reached it after indefinite delays, was a nightmare of dead and dying soldiers. The scene confronting us pushed from my mind reflection, perception, and indeed, thought itself. I knew nothing about nursing and hundreds of wounded soldiers were brought into the American Hospital at Neuilly every day where we had no beds to give them and few remedies to dull their pain. How I wished I had taken even a First Aid Course! My inability to assuage pain soon reduced me to a wraith of my former self and I decided to return to the States. All the way home I slept and though three other women shared the stateroom and talked constantly I could not rouse myself even to fear the dangers of the deep, which they assured me were mounting daily.

Chapter 2

THE HOUND OF HEAVEN

After my disastrous dip into European war work I was more restless than ever. I wanted to run away from everything familiar — to hide somewhere — anywhere — and decided on the White Mountains of New Hampshire where we had remodeled an old abandoned farmhouse. My young daughter Wanden drove a car, and with my usual impatience we darted off. We had passed Newburyport and were rounding the curved beaches of Little Boar's Head when a powerful sedan driven at top speed turned the corner behind us and crashed into our lightly built car reducing it to matchwood. Wanden, though unhurt, was pinned behind the wheel and I was tossed into a watery ditch. A kindly farmer plodding along with a horse and wagon dismounted and carried me into the nearest cottage. Returning, he freed Wanden from the wheel and found the young man who had been trying out the speed of his new car lying in a wood on a bed of pine needles. Though not badly hurt he was too dazed to answer questions or make sense. Our good Samaritan we never knew — neither his name nor where he lived. Virtue had to be its own reward. When I became conscious, late in the afternoon of that day, I was startled to see above my head the picture of 'Abdu'l-Bahá. I felt again the power that had already challenged me to an immortal combat. How strange is Fate! The Hound of Heaven had won the race! Even greater than the pain of a broken ankle was the knowledge that I had turned away from guidance and followed my own will. The will is a stubborn weed. Even as you cut it down it springs to life in a new garden and adorns

7

itself with other colors to deceive you. It took pressure from on high and pressure from within to bend, even to dent, that persistent enemy. "Make of your will a door through which the confirmations of the Holy Spirit may enter," advises 'Abdu'l-Bahá.

The house I had so unexpectedly invaded belonged to my cousin Harry Randall who had rented it for the summer. He, with his wife Ruth, had become Bahá'ís even before 'Abdu'l-Bahá's visit to America in 1912. Harry and Ruth were not only willing but eager to teach me the fundamentals of the Faith during the weeks before I could be moved to New York. Nothing seemed strange to me. It seemed rather as though I had a distant recollection of the Mystic Way: a memory of having known these truths long, long ago. I loved the poetry of the Oriental language even before I understood its symbolism. "The Nightingale of Paradise" was such a satisfying title for One sent down from Heaven to teach us.

When I recovered I accepted the Bahá'í Faith and stood at the foot of that steep ascent that each must travel alone.

Chapter 3

A NEW VISTA

Bahá'í Assemblies as we know them today were not yet functioning. We met at the home of one of the friends to discuss the possibility of having a Bahá'í center. The group seemed to me to lack efficiency — they did not get things done. They needed (in my opinion) more up to date ideas — more go-ahead methods, but when I proposed immediate action they reminded me of the law of consultation. This law that was to play so mighty a part in the future of mankind was new to me and I did not as yet understand it. Then, meditation was another thorn in the flesh — action was my sphere and the idea of meditation disturbed me profoundly, as did the problem of sacrifice. Its appearance in the life of a believer was hailed with high approval, while I had made every effort to avoid sacrifice.

Though fashion was no longer my criterion of character, I was enough of a Philistine to be affected by appearances. The friends went into raptures over a certain woman whose skirts drooped in the back and hiked up in front, and whose hair needed cutting. She was spoken of as "a lovely soul," but for me these trifling defects prevented her soul qualities from shining. I was depressed by the conversations of the Bahá'ís because I knew neither the people nor the events to which they referred. Faith and enthusiasm were met by challenging tests wherever I turned. Mother Beecher, Dorothy Baker's grandmother, was then alive and she, with Hooper Harris, Mary Handford Ford, Saffa Kinney and Grace Krug, helped

9

me over the rough spots and told me of their experiences in
coming into the Faith. The Nineteen Day Feasts, however,
were pure joy. Usually there was a letter that had been received by someone from the Master and this was read aloud —
a breath of heaven reaching us from beyond the seas.

One Feast night Edith Sanderson's plea for someone to
come to Paris was discussed and the post was offered me.
What a land to try one's wings, amid the chestnut blossoms
and the couturiers of the Champs Elysées in Paris! Early the
next month, having gained my husband's consent, I arrived
and found an eminently respectable hotel in a quiet district,
and engaged a large square room on the ground floor in which
to serve tea and discuss the Faith.

Chapter 4

THE LETTER

It was the Spring of 1916 when many Orientals were passing through Paris. The Bahá'ís among them came to the meetings; they sat on the floor along the walls making a frieze with their flowing robes and Biblical head coverings. Animation, characteristic of the West, was totally absent. They remained motionless, smiling often, drinking their tea, but seldom speaking. One afternoon while making the rounds of my Oriental companions, teapot in hand, I noticed a tragic face looking at me from deepset eyes with dark shadows underneath. As he held up his cup, the flowing sleeves fell back, exposing wrists that had been severed through to the bone. I drew back in horror. "What has happened to you?" I asked, pointing to his arms. "I was imprisoned for my Lord — my hands chained above my head." He gave a gentle smile and went on stirring his tea.

When my guests departed I sat down at a table covered, to hide the wear and tear of daily life, by a chenille cloth of many colors. I rested my elbows in its dusty depth and questioned my soul about the Faith I had embraced. Did I know the Manifestation of God, Bahá'u'lláh? Could I have borne the chains and the prison for His sake? I thought of the Apostles of Christ — how they left all things to preach the Gospel. Now I was living in the Day Christ had foretold — a Day prophesied down through the ages — and I saw that I could not follow both the world and the spirit. One or the other I must choose and hold above life itself. Before I could teach others I must come to grips with myself. All night I sat dazed, with these

11

seething thoughts rushing through my brain. When the first
streaks of light penetrated the closed shutters, I seized a pen
and wrote:

"Dear 'Abdu'l-Bahá,
"I think I better go home — I don't know enough about the
Faith to conduct a center and besides, I am not good enough."

I laid the letter on the desk; as there were no letter boxes
then in Paris, I planned to mail it later in the day. Exhausted,
I sat down to drink my morning *cafe au lait* when a visitor was
announced. He was a tall Persian, his name I do not remember, only that he came direct from Haifa, from the presence of
'Abdu'l-Bahá. He drew from beneath his abba a letter addressed to me in the Master's handwriting. I looked longingly
at the thin grey envelope but I could not decipher a word nor
could the bearer help me. Feverishly, I went in search of
Akbar, who had an Oriental shop and spoke both Persian and
English. When I found him, he was engaged with a procras-
tinating customer, who was inspecting every piece of silk
and bric-a-brac in the shop. At last, Akbar bowed him to the
door, sat down and drew the single sheet from the envelope
and read:

"Thy determination to return home is very dear to the
heart of 'Abdu'l-Bahá. The home is the center from which
life radiates to all horizons. Do thou go home and be humble
and be obedient and bye and bye, thou shalt become 'Abdu'l-
Bahá's lion and roar across the Seven Seas."

Breathless, I rushed to the steamship office and engaged a
berth and in a week, I was again on the high sea.

My return home was marked by definite changes. I had a
deeper understanding with my husband and a new sense of
happiness that had nothing to do with events, pervaded me.
The qualities of humility and obedience, mentioned by 'Abdu'l-
Bahá in his letter, were rusty from disuse and to ingraft them
on my rebellious nature I turned to the Bahá'í Prayer Book in
quest of help and memorized a prayer.

"Is there any Remover of difficulties save God? Say: Praised be God! He is God! All are His servants, and all abide by His bidding!
— The Báb

I had climbed another step up the steep mountain of spiritual understanding and the panorama of life widened and took on new beauty.

Chapter 5

WAR AND HUMAN NATURE

The United States joined the Allies, entering the war on April 6, 1917. A cry went up for workers and both my family and the Bahá'ís urged me to offer my services. My husband could not go as he was under heavy financial responsibility, so for the third time during World War I, I set out across the Atlantic bound for Mission Ambrine, the only hospital for the treatment of the burned, and one that followed close behind the lines. It was stationed at Compeigne near the glorious forest now touched with green through which sunlight filtered making checkered shadows on the paths. Here, where Kings and Queens, and courtiers with princely retinues once walked, were now the grim evidences of war — the square in front of the palace that had spread its magnificence for the admiration of all Europe was filled with ammunition and over the ridge at Noyen the guns fired ceaselessly, night and day.

The Mission had been financed by Madame X who belonged to one of the well-known families of Europe and who was part French and part Austrian. She was the head of the Mission and I was the foot — the kitchen maid, so to speak. This lovely position gave me opportunity to watch the criss-cross motives that actuate human nature. I learned to recognize the ways of the worldly, the methods used by the envious, the obvious plays of the stupid and the goodness of the pure of heart. Long hours of work combined with scanty diet helped to make me a sturdy soldier and I owe much to the months that I spent in the Mission. Madame X was not fond of me, and failing to draw me into her train of admirers, decided to

15

punish me now and then. But as a boomerang, the darts pierced her own breast and I recollect one delicious occasion. Two great burning ambitions actuated the personnel. The first was to have Generals Petain and the high-ups visit the hospital, which they had never done; and the next was to be invited to the British Headquarters at Amiens. Finally an invitation came through for the staff to lunch at Amiens. That day Madame X turned to me and said sweetly, "Someone must stay at home, and as there is no grave case in the hospital I have decided to leave you."

My punishment was light. I was able to take a bath (a rare luxury) and arrived at the hospital in the pink of condition. During the afternoon, the soldiers came running across the corridor exclaiming breathlessly that the Great Generals were approaching. "Show them in" said I, in the grand manner. And looking up I saw the glittering medals shining on the breasts of General Petain, Joffre and Pershing. I bowed low and they bent their noble backs in my direction. I inquired if they cared to see the hospital, to which proposition they amicably agreed. There were a thousand beds and the treatment salons occupied half a block. General Pershing seemed affected by finding this mammoth establishment under the care of a small American woman — I neither accepted nor repudiated the implication — I simply passed it by as became one in my station. I had heard that Petain was fond of chocolate and I had a package from home which I instructed the soldiers to prepare. We sat in the small refectory chatting, sipping America's best and nibbling sweet biscuits. They seemed in no hurry to depart and when they finally left, expressed no end of pleasure for their afternoon tea party.

Darkness had fallen when our ancient and springless camion drew up in the courtyard. Limp and stiff from the long drive and covered with dust from the shell pitted roads, they descended one by one, Madame X the last, looking pale as a ghost and grey with fatigue. "Well," she said, "have you anything to report?" I took a long breath before exploding the bombshell: "Only that three Generals came to see the hospital and had tea."

Anguish wracked her frame but all she said in a tragic tone was: "You may go to bed!"

Full of chocolate and compliments I departed. Bed! It was the top luxury of the war! The perfect reward and compensation for all one's efforts — she had bestowed the golden ending to a perfect day.

Chapter 6

ON LEAVE IN PARIS

Again that winter I played the role of Cinderella on a twenty-four hour leave in Paris. I usually stayed with two American friends of long standing. Arriving at Rue Thiers, an astonishing sight met my eyes! A snow-storm of tissue paper obscured the furniture, jewel cases lay open on the beds, and from the closet door hung a Worth evening gown with its train billowing over the carpet. A train — that prehistoric appendage outlawed since 1914! What could have brought about such a collection of forbidden goods! Sisters Mary and Joan explained the mystery. There was to be given, tonight at the British Embassy, a dinner for General Lawrence of Arabia. "We can't ask you," sister Mary said, "as the list of guests was made out at the legation and includes only distinguished people and a few like ourselves who live in Paris." "Don't mind me," I rejoined gaily. "I have nothing with me but the uniform I am wearing, and anyway I promised to dine with Lt. Verry who knows no one here — has very little money and only a short leave from the trenches."

Lt. Verry was a gallant figure who had come from New Caledonia to fight side by side with the French of his ancestors. Nomea, on the other side of the world, was written on his identity bracelet. He had found an inconspicuous cafe, the Chat Dorée, advertising chicken on Thursdays. At the front, food was a basic theme of conversation and a gnawing want every hour of the day, since our menu of black bread and horse meat was only varied by an occasional potato or bit of cabbage for Sunday dinner. There was but one waiter in the Chat

19

Dorée and he eyed our uniforms and evidently regarded us as comrades-in-arms and delighted to have a chance to express his views on current affairs. He permitted himself a bit of sarcasm as to the management of the war in general and the supervision of food in particular. With a grand flourish he deposited a leg of chicken on each plate and leaning over my shoulder whispered, "See that man in the corner with a book against the carafe?" We gazed in the direction of his waving napkin and saw a man in an unfamiliar uniform without stripe or decoration or any mark by which he could be identified. "That," continued our informant, "is General Lawrence of Arabia."

There sat the Lion! Alone and not concerned that ambassadors and ladies, arrayed like the lilies of the field, awaited him. In this unknown spot was the man of mystery whose exploits had challenged the world, and whose adventures rivaled the Arabian Nights. "Go and ask if we may join him for coffee," Verry said. We could see him nod his head without raising his eyes from the book. We walked over and sat down. He evinced not the slightest curiosity as to our identity. Stirring his coffee, he remarked that he considered it the best coffee in Paris and that he always came here when passing through. We spoke of our uniforms being uncomfortable and he replied that the oriental dress was far more practical than European clothes. "I will never make a real soldier," he said, laughing, "for I haven't learned the first rule — obedience." It was hard to keep from exclaiming that he was the greatest soldier of the war but we mastered the temptation and having drained the last drop of coffee from our cups we withdrew.

I returned to the house of the sisters where the glittering robes were being laid away in camphor.

"Well, how was your Lion?" I asked, malice mingled with the sugar. "He wasn't there — at the last moment he was called to London for a war conference." "No doubt," I countered, "that he left Paris for London, but he did have time to take a cup of coffee with us at the Chat Dorée before he embarked."

Chapter 7

ROYALTY ADRIFT

The French peasants of the devastated villages were hungry and destitute and the Red Cross decided to give a grand fete in their aid. It was held in a lovely garden in the Bois de Bologne and the nurses from the Mission were sent to Paris to help. We were nearly as hungry as the peasants and welcomed the opportunity to pass frosted cakes and sugared cookies, so we could steal a mouthful every now and again. Here I met the Grand Duke Dimitri, who told me he wanted to go to America and study with Mrs. Cocheran whose science of numbers greatly interested him.

"Did you ever hear of the Bahá'í Faith," I queried, "for she is a Bahá'í and so am I." He questioned me at length about the Faith and I spoke of the Tablet Bahá'u'lláh had sent to the Duke's grandfather warning him of disintegration in his kingdom and of the necessity of becoming aware of the identity of Bahá'u'lláh. Dimitri was deeply impressed in learning that the first Bahá'í Temple was erected in Russia. He said he had heard of 'Abdu'l-Bahá but he could not remember where, and I related how the Russian Consul in Haifa had offered refuge to him when a delegation of Turkish soldiers arrived to put him to death. The Master had refused to save himself, he said neither the Báb nor Bahá'u'lláh had fled from their enemies nor should he — if God willed that he die, he was ready. Dimitri explained that he had been exiled from Russia for his part in the murder of Rasputin. A few men feared Rasputin's power and determined to rid the country of his presence; a banquet

21

of great magnificence had been staged on New Year's Eve of last year (1916). The place chosen was the house of Prince Yousoupov on the Moila, in Petrograd; after repeated attempts they had finally silenced the arch-enemy.

Dimitri said, "You are fortunate to have a Faith to cling to — I have none." I drew from my purse a tiny Bahá'í pamphlet and gave it to him. Absent-mindedly he put it in his pocket and turned away. In a few minutes he was back. "Perhaps you have a prayer or something that would rid me of Rasputin's evil eyes that follow me everywhere. Try and send me something," he said in a tragic tone, and laid an address on the tea table and was gone.

Shortly after our meeting Dimitri was interned by the English and during that period the Royal family of Russia, as well as the four Grand Dukes, were executed. Dimitri became the rightful heir to the throne. I wrote to the address he had given me, enclosing Bahá'í prayers and quotations. I had a single line from him before the close of the war. It said, "I am unhappy in England — it is dark — pray for me."

When war ended and Dimitri was free, the Bolsheviki had come into power and it was evident that he would never see his homeland again. He made a futile effort to re-enter life by marrying an American girl but it proved a failure and soon he fell ill and died.

This incident vividly impressed on my mind the fateful words of Bahá'u'lláh:

> "The world's equilibrium hath been upset through the vibrating influence of this most great, this new World Order. Mankind's ordered life hath been revolutionized through the agency of this unique, this wondrous System — the like of which mortal eyes have never witnessed."

Chapter 8

THE CANTEEN AT LAON

When it was evident that war would soon end, engineers were sent to rebuild the roads and bridges that led to Laon. Early in the war the Germans had captured the city and held it. Volunteers were called to open a canteen and with three other nurses I went. The town overlooked the Chemin des Dames, that road over which the court of Medieval days had travelled and from which it took its name "Road of the Ladies." Recent battles on its exposed rampart had been bloody and disastrous.

We were billeted in a shell-torn villa, the windows nailed with rough boards, leaving us only one for light. The floor was covered with clanking planks and there was no heat. Our one joy was the canteen that boasted a gas log and a stove for making tea or coffee.

One afternoon as we were dressing to leave our wind-swept quarters, someone said it was snowing and we rushed to the window. The snow was light and swirling in the wind but looking down on the Chemin des Dames we saw a stalled motor with four soldiers working in frantic haste. One was rolling a tire, another was jacking up the wheel and two were taking something from the back of the disabled car. Two French soldiers were on the floor below and we asked them to come up and see what they thought was going on. Looking from the window one remarked, "They are certainly working at top speed. It gets me where they think they are going — they are at the end of the road now."

"Wherever they are going we must give them some coffee

at the canteen. Will you boys go down and ask them up?" The soldiers, always good tempered, trotted off and were soon lost to view. We waited until we heard a shout from the lane below our window, then hurried to hear the news. "What do you think! We went all the way down there, but there wasn't a soul! Not a sign of anybody on the road." "There was no camion either," chimed in the other soldier.

We stood there amazed, "You mean to say that the soldiers we were watching were not there?"

"That's right. It was as silent as the grave."

"The weirdest thing of all," reflected the second soldier, "there were no marks of wheels on the road. The dust is thick and I should say nothing had been over that road for days."

Six pairs of eyes had been focused on what? A mirage? We had no answer. Edith Blake, our most analytical observer, recalled that in *Outward Bound,* where all the characters are dead, none knew it and even when the evidence presented was overwhelming they refused to believe the truth. From World War II we have two books written by men of wide reputation that help to clarify this experience. In the first, *Falling through Space,* the author Paul Fleming writes:

> "Though I was lying in a London hospital with eyes bandaged, I nevertheless witnessed the death of my comrade Paul. I saw a luft-waffe come out of the clouds behind Paul's machine and fire directly at him. I screamed a warning (which naturally he did not hear). For one moment the plane remained motionless and then slowly turned over and fell."

And Antoine de Saint Exupéry in *Flight Over Arras* has given us this magnificent statement:

> "Man when dying sees that he will not be cut off from his kind, but will make himself one with them. He would not be losing himself, but finding himself. This is a truth hidden under the veneer of our everyday illusion. But in the instant when you are giving up your body, you learn to your amazement . . . how little store you set by your body. It would be foolish to deny that during all those years of my life when nothing insistent was prompting me . . . that nothing was half so important as

my body. But here in this plane I say to my body 'I don't care a button what becomes of you. There is no hope of your surviving this and yet I lack nothing. In the past it was not I who thought, not I who felt; it was you; my body.' "

The girls turned to me and said, "Perhaps you have something to tell us of eternal life from your Bahá'í Teachings." I rummaged in my duffle-bag and brought out a small compilation on Life Eternal, wherein, 'Abdu'l-Bahá writes:

"The human condition may be likened to the womb of the mother from which a child is to be born into the spacious outer world. At first the infant finds it very difficult to reconcile itself to its new existence. It is reluctant to leave its home but nature forces it into this world. Having come into its new condition it finds that it has passed from darkness into a sphere of radiance; from gloomy and restricted surroundings it has been transferred to an environment spacious and delightful. This analogy expresses the relation of the temporal world to the life hereafter; the transition of the soul of man from darkness and uncertainty to the light and reality of the eternal Kingdom. At first it is difficult to welcome death but after attaining its new condition the soul is grateful for its release from the bondage of the limited to enjoy the liberties of the unlimited."

We forgot we were cold and hungry. We forgot we were due at the canteen — nothing seemed important in the light of the strange event that had taken place before our eyes.

When next in Paris I went to Miss Sanderson's apartment. Edith, from time to time, sent a collective letter from us to 'Abdu'l-Bahá and I added what I had seen and asked what it meant. The Master replied that the soldiers had been catapulted out of life with such sudden force that they did not realize their changed condition. That since they were deprived of their earth experience through no fault of their own, God would, in the future compensate them and give them their hearts' desires.

Chapter 9

DR. ESSLEMONT

The war that was to end all war was over! How little we knew! I came to Paris from Laon to await my turn for a passage to New York in one of the few boats left afloat. I found my former room vacant and walked in. The table covered by the same rainbow hues welcomed me; I gave it a pat of recognition since it had shared the dark night of my soul. At last I was a Bahá'í — loyalties conserved, aims focused, and the future Bahá'í plan a bit clearer. I was happy and often my heart sang like a lark on the wing. Work had toughened my fiber and reduced my ego. To have nothing to do was pure joy and as I sat dreaming in my rocking chair, luxuriating in idleness, the door opened and Dr. Esslemont walked in. I had never seen him before and how Scotch he was! Unruly red hair, freckles and wide-awake brown eyes. From his tweed coat was slung a worn briefcase in which was the manuscript of *Bahá'u'lláh and the New Era* — that little volume that has gone round the world and been translated into nearly a hundred languages. I begged him to tell me about his visit to the Master — how he came to go and what was his life while near to 'Abdu'l-Bahá. We drew our chairs close to the open grate. Very simply he told his story:

He was a physician in charge of a sanatorium in Bournemouth for tubercular cases, and he made frequent journeys to London to consult the directors of the hospital. Usually he glanced over the morning paper and snipped from it any article that appealed to him. He had heard of the Bahá'í Faith from several people and was much struck by its answers to the

27

problems of the day and had made a few notes about it for his own use. Therefore he had torn from the paper the talk given by 'Abdu'l-Bahá the day before at the London Temple. A man sitting near said that he was going to hear this famous Oriental at Lady Bloomfield's that afternoon and they decided to go together. The Master gave a short talk on Bahá'u'lláh's Teachings and afterwards, while Esslemont was hesitating whether to go forward, the interpreter tapped him on the shoulder and said the Master wished to speak to him. Esslemont followed his guide through the milling crowd to where 'Abdu'l-Bahá stood.

The Master greeted him kindly and as though it was the most natural thing in the world, said: "Dr. Esslemont, I would like you to write Bahá'u'lláh's Message for the Western world." Before the Doctor could protest that he knew nothing of His Message, 'Abdu'l-Bahá continued, "It would be necessary for you to come to Haifa and visit me." The Doctor was so taken by surprise that he stammered that that was quite impossible. 'Abdu'l-Bahá replied, smiling, "When the right time comes, it will be quite easy."

The Master turned away to reply to someone else. In a strange perplexity of mind the Doctor returned to Bournemouth, the words 'Abdu'l-Bahá had spoken ringing in his mind. Why had he been thus addressed — what could it mean? His whole being was churned up and sleep retreated from his eyes for many nights.

Three years later Esslemont had a hemorrhage of the lungs and the directors of the Sanatorium, fearful of losing him, offered him a vacation and urged him to go to a warmer clime. The Master's invitation loomed large before his eyes and on impulse he sent a cable: "I am free to come to Haifa if you still want me." The answer came promptly, "Come to Haifa. 'Abdu'l-Bahá is expecting you." Thus he entered a new world — the world of perfection. He had never imagined such sacrifice, such beauty of character, such heavenly conduct as he now witnessed.

One day 'Abdu'l-Bahá took him to the tomb of Bahá'u'lláh and allowed him to enter alone. Jasmine and roses twined among the columns of the Tomb. The birds flew in and out. Esslemont knelt on one of the steps — a strange calm enveloped him. His former life with its happenings seemed swept away — like wax his spirit melted and was made ready for a new image. The perfume from the flowers pervaded the atmosphere and he was so lost to the outer world that when the Master tapped him on the shoulder, he came back as from a far country. After the experience in the Tomb of Bahá'u'lláh, the panorama of the plan for the Faith was understood by him without let or hindrance. The glory that surrounded the person of 'Abdu'l-Bahá drew him higher and higher as the days passed: those never-to-be-forgotten dawns during which they wended their way to the poor quarters of the city; 'Abdu-l-Bahá entering a hovel as though it were the palace of a king. He cooked gruel, washed the sick, swept the floor and spoke words of comfort to each — not outward comfort, but words that answered the needs of the heart. The Master walked so swiftly that Esslemont could scarcely keep pace with him. Returning home, 'Abdu'l-Bahá would join the family for tea, chant the prayers and when the sun rose he would be ready for the duties of the day. Most difficult of all is to describe the Master! A harmony filled his being and light seemed to radiate from every motion he made.

All night we sat before the dying embers, Esslemont trying to give me a picture of the heaven he had been privileged to enter. His words poured over me, but alas, afterwards I remembered only a fraction of what he said. At six in the morning his train left for Calais and as we said goodbye I begged him to pray that I too might understand the root of the Bahá'í Teachings and follow in his footsteps. "Someone from the other world will help you." He pressed my hand and was gone.

How often in my mind's eye have I seen the little grave on the side of Mt. Carmel where Esslemont lies; how often have

I felt his bright spirit near me, helping me to understand the mysteries enshrined in the Faith!

Chapter 10

THE BOUNTY

At this period a momentous chapter of Bahá'í history was being enacted in Haifa for 'Abdu'l-Bahá was sending his eldest grandson to the University of Oxford in England. The event entailed far more than outer happening for in reality 'Abdu'l-Bahá was bidding an earthly farewell to him whom he had chosen to become the first Guardian of the Faith (that well-guarded secret). The parting severed the companionship since his birth of Shoghi Effendi Rabbani with the Master and though the Master shielded him from actual knowledge, when I remember the sadness reflected in his dark eyes I believe a presentiment clouded his sensitive soul.

To break the long journey Shoghi Effendi Rabbani and Dr. Lutfu'lláh Hakím stopped with me in Paris and Oh! how little I realized who was beneath my roof! How little I knew the inestimable; the unbelievable bounty that had been bestowed upon me!

Part Two

Lights and Shadows Cross the Path

Chapter 11

NEW IDEAS

I came home. This time for good. Never, never, I vowed, would I cross the wicked old Atlantic again. My intention, real at the moment, was short-lived. Friends crowded round me to hear my war experiences. They were curious, too, about my new religion.

"Do you say different prayers from ours?" I was right in my element since I had learned only recently these things for myself. "Yes, we have prayers for every occasion — many more than I knew existed." Meditation is of prime importance too — what can happen from meditation is a miracle — I don't remember it all but this is what 'Abdu'l-Bahá says in part:

> "Meditation is the key for opening the doors of the mysteries . . . This faculty brings forth the sciences and arts from the invisible plane . . . Through the meditative faculty inventions are made possible, colossal undertakings are carried out . . . affairs of which man knew nothing are unfolded."

Another thing we learn is that work is a form of worship. Lady Bloomfield in her book *The Chosen Highway* relates the following incident while 'Abdu'l-Bahá was visiting her in London:

> "A workman who had left his bag of tools in the hall was welcomed with smiling kindness by 'Abdu'l-Bahá. With a look of sadness the man said: 'I don't know much about religious things, as I have no time for anything but work.' 'That is well. A day's work done in the spirit of service is in itself an act of worship. Such work is a prayer unto God.' The man's face cleared from its shadow of doubt and hesitation and he went from the Master's presence happy and strengthened."

"Well," someone said, "that is a new idea — I have to think about that." And another said "I like to make up my own prayers." "But," I replied, "your words have not the power of those of a Messenger of God. You must think when saying The Lord's Prayer that it is more powerful than anything you can compose." So the discussions would leap from one subject to another and by explaining the Cause to my friends I learned to give the Message.

It was at this time that I first met Marion Little. She had been overseas with the Red Cross and we had our European experiences in common. A bond of understanding affection sprang up between us — a bond that has lasted through the years. Marion would come from her interior decorating work, throw herself down on an immense high-backed sofa, known in the family as "the universal bed," and from its depths we would discuss everything under the sun. But, no matter at what point the conversation began, it veered to religion and to the Bahá'í Faith specifically. From the first, Marion was attracted to the Teachings — her heart was convinced even before she studied, and it was not long before we were walking hand and hand — two new and eager Bahá'ís. Her services in the European field of pioneering today are widely known, but in those early days there were many questions that baffled us — one in particular: How much free will has man? A letter written to a German believer by 'Abdu'l-Bahá was received in America by Mr. Pauli about this time and helped us understand this abstruse matter. I will give it here in my own words: Man cannot choose the century in which he will be born, he cannot choose his antecedents or his parents, neither the country, religion nor environment into which he comes. These are termed by 'Abdu'l-Bahá "the ground threads of life." An English Bahá'í wrote the Master this question: "Why am I born an English woman of the nineteenth century and a Christian instead of being born a man, a Chinese, a follower of Confucius in the Middle ages?" 'Abdu'l-Bahá replied that this was one of the three great mysteries of this plane — the riddle of free will. He then went on to tell her what we could do with free will. When man arrives on earth he finds the ground threads ready — the loom of life set up. The soul takes the shuttle and chooses its own pattern. Sometimes it employs beautiful colors and silken threads and creates a masterpiece; or uses coarse threads and weaves a crude design. Sometimes there is no mark on the frame of life. Many begin a plan — become discouraged and abandon it, seize another idea but cannot carry it to completion; so when life ends there stands the frame covered with fragments.

Again 'Abdu'l-Bahá gives us another symbol in the track and the engine. The track is immovable (our birth and the conditions surrounding it) but the engineer (the soul) may go fast or slow, he may switch onto other tracks or not, as he chooses; stop at way stations or pass them by. He can obey the traffic laws or ignore them. What shall we do about this puzzling matter? 'Abdu'l-Bahá advises: find a harmony between the free and not-free happenings of life, between the conscious and the unconscious will; seek to make the will conform to the Divine Will, then man possesses the greatest treasure: indestructible peace of mind.

Chapter 12

WHO SHALL BE FIRST

One morning Grace Krug telephoned me that a letter had arrived from the Master regarding the forming of an Assembly. We were to meet at her apartment that evening to study the instructions and she had cabled 'Abdu'l-Bahá of our intentions. The novelty of the situation brought us together in a state of excitement, since no Assembly had as yet been formed in New York. We knew little of procedure. We pretended to each other to be aware how to go about it and we bustled around trying to appear important and official. We felt the thing to do was to impress each other that we had special understanding and were favored with unique knowledge. First we sat along the wall in a row, stiff and upright. Then someone suggested that such a formation was not conducive to the flow of the spirit, so we formed a circle, being careful to pull our chairs in exact relation to that of our neighbor. All of a sudden there was a loud peal from the doorbell. Grace sprang to answer the summons, as though she knew what was on the other side of the partition. She returned waving a cablegram — a message from 'Abdu'l-Bahá. The circle vibrated with agitation. Breathless, we waited while Grace drew the yellow sheet from its envelope. Adjusting her glasses, she read us the contents: "Read Matthew, Chapter 19, Verse 30." Where is the Bible? There on the lower shelf, no, try the top shelf — is there a stepladder! The Scriptures were finally run to earth. Grace thumbed through the pages and lo, here was the verse! "But many that are first shall be last; and the last shall be first."

Presto, we became as humble as mice — afraid lest that last place should be ours! 'Abdu'l-Bahá gave us a wonderful lesson that evening! If we went away without too much knowledge of how to form an Assembly, we learned a lesson in how to become Bahá'ís. Bathed in the aura of humility the Assembly came into being. The spiced breezes of endeavor blew over the land.

Chapter 13

JENABI FAZEL

In April, 1920, 'Abdu'l-Bahá sent Jenabi Fazel to teach in America. Of him the Master wrote, he had perfections — plural. Here then was a man with the aura of many virtues — not a single quality of goodness but a cluster of bright stars shining. He was above average height and powerfully built. His dark eyes radiated light and he was crowned by a white turban. He did not speak English but imparted his thoughts just the same. I remember a luncheon when he arranged the black seeds of a watermelon in circles, to explain the simile between the rising sun of the physical world and the rise of the spiritual Suns. Fazel chanted the prayers and though many of the friends were familiar with the chant I had never heard it. It is pitched in a high, somewhat nasal, tone that produces a sense of nostalgia, it makes the sound seem to come from afar like the call from a minaret. It gave me a peculiar sensation at first and then I grew to respond to its special quality and to love it.

One day Fazel expressed a desire to see one of the series of educational films then being shown by the public schools of New York. I was entranced not only to go with him but to go alone instead of in a troupe. His mind was so deep and clear that just to be in his presence was a privilege. We went. The showing was *Relativity* by Albert Einstein. As each symbol appeared in white on a black drop, Fazel repeated "Very good, very good," and smiled tenderly. It was immensely interesting and I enjoyed it. When it terminated, I reached for my coat, feeling a bit hungry, as it was noon. Fazel looked shocked

41

— "Not go," he said, "we stay, we see." We sat down again and remained in our seats until the last showing was over. I do not remember the number of times the film was shown but I think five or six. Smiling, relaxed, and happy, Fazel sat hour after hour drinking in the broad theory of Mr. Einstein. When the curtain descended with "The End" written on it, Fazel sighed, and we arose. I was cramped, cold, hungry and exhausted but Fazel was fresh as a spring morning. Since that time whenever a conversation turns upon the theories of Einstein I boldly assert that I know ALL ABOUT Relativity.

Chapter 14

'ABDU'L-BAHÁ LEAVES US

At this period a horde of unemployed roved the streets of New York and the Bahá'ís were assisting Dr. Guthrie at St. Mark's Episcopal Church with a soup kitchen he had established. He, in return, allowed us to use the lovely little Chapel for our Bahá'í Commemorations. It was Monday, November 28, 1921. We were busy dismantling the decorations of fruit, vegetables and autumn leaves that had garnished the church for Thanksgiving. I was on top of a stepladder untwining long green branches that hung above the pulpit. Looking down, I saw Mountfort Mills standing at the door. I heard the words he uttered in a low, impassioned voice: "'Abdu'l-Bahá passed away this morning at about half past one."

It rushed over me that I had not gone to Haifa! I had never seen 'Abdu'l-Bahá! This awful thought engulfed me, flowed over me in waves of sorrow. I felt myself catapulted out onto the rim of existence. I remember nothing of the intervening hours between the time of Mountfort's heartbreaking announcement and the moment that I found myself sitting in St. Mark's listening to the reading of the Will of 'Abdu'l-Bahá. As his words of admonition and advice poured out, there fell upon my ears the words of healing, words of comfort:

> "O my loving friends! After the passing away of this wronged one, it is incumbent upon . . . the loved ones of the Abhá Beauty to turn unto Shoghi Effendi . . . the youthful Branch . . . branched from the two Hallowed and Sacred Lote-Trees . . . He is the Sign of God, the Chosen Branch, the Guardian of the Cause of God."

Thus from that hour did Shoghi Effendi become to us all what the words of 'Abdu'l-Bahá implied: our Most Beloved Guardian.

43

Chapter 15

PORTOFINO LIBRARY

Opening a letter in the morning mail a check fluttered to the floor — a check for five hundred dollars! It was difficult to take my hypnotized eyes off the check long enough to read the accompanying note. It was from Elinor Stewart, a kind and loving friend who was at the time studying the Bahá'í Principles. She heard we were to establish a religious library in Portofino, Italy — a library from which we could send books all over Europe. I had already cabled the Guardian to ask if we should send only Bahá'í books. His answer was to include the sacred books of all religions. For this we needed advice and as Mr. Brentano, Senior, was then alive, we consulted him. His enthusiasm equalled ours. He chose gems of philosophic thought, treatises on the inner life, essays on the ancient beliefs, many volumes unknown to us that proved of inestimable value in the library. The high adventure was set afloat on the S.S. *Guilio Cesare* and in due time the books arrived intact and were installed at the Villa San Martino. A dull red shade was chosen for the cover of the catalogue with the Tree of Knowledge spreading over Bahá'u'lláh's Words:
  "The root of all knowledge is the knowledge of God."
From catalogues of universities and school libraries we compiled a mailing list and the Tree of Knowledge went forth! Responses appeared from many quarters of Europe, among them a note from Germany, scarcely legible: "Your catalogue at hand. We see you have *Cosmic Consciousness*. This book, the only one in the women's prison of Moscow, has passed

45

through so many hands that fifty pages (those between 40 and 90) are illegible. If you have time to copy these pages, send them to this address, and we will see that they are translated and reach Lubin prison of Russia. They will be acknowledged by means of a small x." No letter x appeared in the mail that summer but the following spring, while standing on the terrace of San Martino, Rosa, our impeccable housekeeper who went with the Villa, came running from the front door. "Senora, there is a man downstairs — not a caller I assure you — a poor, untidy man, a beggar I presume, he won't give me a message" — but I was already on my way to the door and Rosa turned her back to avoid witnessing such impropriety.

There stood a man, bearing out Rosa's description — he was not only shabby but deep lines of despair were written on his pale face. He stood looking at me but saying not a word. I felt faintly worried as I inquired what I could do for him.

"I have come from Russia and I have with me a package for you." He held out something wrapped in tattered newspaper. "I must reach Genoa and a ship, tonight." So saying, he backed towards the entrance and was gone. I had forgotten the Russian prison and now it came back to me as I drew the newspaper away. Inside was a mat, about the size of a saucer and with it a note written in English: "The women of the Moscow prison received your priceless gift. We wish we had something real to send you but here, we have nothing. Someone had hidden from the guards a bit of string — our only possession. Each one pricked her finger to redden the string and with our only hairpin we have woven a mat. We send it to you by a trusted friend." There in the corner was the symbol that I was to look for — a small x.

"I am teaching school," wrote Miss Crandall, "and am boarding at a fruit farm on the African veldt. The house is Dutch in design, surrounded by high white walls. In this part of the world fruit trees are trained, espaliered against the walls and look more like vines than trees. When the peaches and pears are ripening the brilliancy of color defies description. Beside myself there is an ill-fated hunting expedition, marooned here,

as one man has a broken leg, another has a lacerated hand and
their companions are loathe to leave them. The catalogue has
sent them into spasms of delight and they keep shouting at me
their requests as I write, we are all agreed that we want *Variety
of Religious Experience* by William James. One man, a Catholic, would like *Fabiola* by Cardinal Wiseman. Another wants
The Light of Asia by Edwin Arnold, and I should like *Foundations of World Unity* and *Divine Art of Living* in order to continue my Bahá'í reading. Unless you have never lived where
books are scarce you could not understand our thirst for the
printed page."

Fifty volumes were wrapped in waterproof paper and
shipped. Considerable time elapsed before we received news
of their arrival. I cite Miss Crandall's letter:

"When we were apprised from Capetown that the books await
us, we went wild. Our Dutch landlord informed the supervisor
of the district and he declared a week's holiday so that the
neighboring farmers might avail themselves of a visit to the
big town. It is a journey of fifty miles winding through mountain roads: one that is unsafe for horses so eighteen mules were
yoked to the one ceremonial wagon the town possesses. We
spent hours decorating it with pieces of bunting and sprigs of
colored leaves cut from the fruit trees. Off we went — a gay
company, singing and cheering as we ambled along the dusty
roads. Men from the fields came running, curious to know
what the festivity was about and many joined us — a break in
the monotonous routine of field work was welcomed and they
hopped in just as they were. By the time we clattered over the
cobblestones of the Capetown wharf we were packed like
sardines in a can. Triumphant, we bore our precious cargo
home and now behold! On the long oaken table are spread
rows of books, just to read their titles gives us a thrill. They
act as life savers for this little colony, marooned on a lonely
African plain. Paeans of thanksgiving from us all."

The most startling experience resulting from the Portofino
Library came from a Madame X, an American who had married an Oriental. The marriage had been a tragic failure from
which she seemed unable to extricate herself. She loved the
Bahá'í meetings but never came to grips with the Faith. After
listening attentively to the explanation on some point, she

would look up with a child-like expression and say: "But why?
I can't see why!" So when she wrote me from Vittel in the
Vosges mountains for a book on the Bahá'í teachings, I confess
I was at a loss to know what to send. I went to the bookcase,
closed my eyes and said The Greatest Name; I put out my
hand and drew down a book. It was *The Divine Art of Living*.
Her reaction was so extraordinary that I give it in her own
words.

Vittel, Vosges Mountains
France
August 6, 1928

Dear friend:

I woke early this morning and as I opened my eyes I remembered that there was something to wake up for — the little
book from the library of Portofino. I was attracted by the title.
It sounded like a definite path to travel and liberated a pent up
force within me. Vistas of becoming a useful human being
showed me there were a hundred answers to my questions.
No doubt dark days will return, but, by opening the little book
cobwebs that cloud my mind will melt away. The joy I have
sought has been centered in earthly love and that love has
brought me dark and tragic moments that increased my loneliness and shattered my nerves. I am unable to recover any
degree of poise after such turbid phases of emotion. Today,
I have new hope — new inspiration and for this no thanks is
adequate for the gift from the Portofino Library.

Lovingly,
Mabel

In the same mail came a second letter still more remarkable:

"You will be surprised, dear friend, to receive a second letter
since I posted one to you this morning, but when you read this
I feel sure you will understand why it had to be written today.
I dropped my first letter to you in a mail box at the entrance
of the hotel and wended my way into the hills that surround
Vittel. Coming upon a green bench I sat down. The view was
in no way remarkable. A road runs to the north, in the sky
were a few fluffy clouds and back of me a hillside covered with
dusty white flowers. Twenty-five kilometers down the road is
the birthplace of Joan d'Arc; it is the same type of country.

I wondered about Joan — so young with no intimation of the terrible fate awaiting her! After a few minutes I opened the little book at random and read: 'Wish for no other companion save the true one. Do ye not desire other associates save turning thy face towards the supreme Horizon.'

"I wanted to think about these words and what they meant to me. I let the book fall on the bench and fastened my eyes on the road. Suddenly between the earth and my eyes, there rose long luminous vibrations of light that increased in intensity until I could no longer see the earth. The light rose higher and higher until it filled all space. It seemed to come from within as well as from without. I was part of the vibration. I could not move nor even lift my hand — I do not know how long it was until the light diminished and I was able to turn my head and look about me. Everything was changed — the hillside, the road, even the sky, each leaf, each blade of grass was rimmed with light. The small white flowers had stars of light at their centers. The very dust of the road sparkled as with diamonds and the clouds were crossed by bands of gold. I wanted to remain forever amid the glories surrounding me, but, I knew I should be missed and must return. I dreaded to find myself enclosed in my bedroom, crowded with ugly furniture — but as I turned the key in the door I saw the table-cloth edged with light as was every single object in the room. Why such another world experience should come to me I cannot understand. Why should I be caught up from my drab life into beauty that is hidden, hidden from our physical eyes? Why should I see light as a cause instead of an effect that I shall never understand. Please send another book — something that might help explain the strange experience through which I have passed.

Mabel"

Experiences of Saints of many lands were packed and sent to the country of Joan d'Arc to companion our traveller on her celestial journeyings.

Chapter 16

THE LEPER COLONY

In 1931 we were invited to spend Christmas in Honolulu. It was the first of many visits paid to that enchanted Isle. With equal truth might the immortal line inscribed on the walls of Delhi Fort have been written for the Island of Oahu: "If there is a paradise on earth, it is here! It is here! It is here!"

Nothing in this magic land required effort. The multicolored hibiscus flower lived exactly as well when laid on a table as when plunged in water. Coconuts dropped from the trees to quench thirst; the sea was warm and without alarm; the sun shone while showers fell filling the valleys with liquid sunshine and causing rainbows to form over hill and dale. The stress and struggle of life faded from one's mind like a dream and in looking backward one marveled at the energy required for daily living in other climes.

The Bahá'ís of Honolulu gave me a warm welcome and asked me to speak at their public meetings. I wondered if 'Abdu'l-Bahá would not have found work to do here — he would not have been content to bask in sunshine — he would have ferreted out someone needy or ill and would have ministered to their needs. Thoughts such as these made me restless. Christmas was approaching; delectable toys filled the shop windows but who was there to give them to?

One night at dinner I sat beside the Governor and asked if there were no poor in Honolulu. Off-hand even he could not think of any. Later in the evening he called me aside: "Why don't you dress a Christmas tree for the leper children?"

51

"Would I catch it, maybe?" With all my zeal I had not reckoned on rubbing shoulders with leprosy.

"No," he replied laughing, "they haven't got it, they are born of mothers in the leper colony of Molokai. Immediately after birth they are flown to Honolulu and placed in charge of the Sisters of Charity. They are brought up as wards of the Islands. We don't wish to alarm our visitors, or disturb our own people, so they are almost unknown. Sad little scraps of humanity they are; I don't believe they know what a toy looks like."

I set to work with a will and with such overflowing energy that money poured in for the celebration. By Christmas Eve there stood a six-foot tree glittering with gold and silver ornaments and toys. There were little carts filled with removable ice cubes and iron tongs to lift them with. There were ponies with coats of real hair and leather harnesses that buckled on. There were dolls of every nation and ballerinas that pirouetted till you grew dizzy watching; not to speak of teddy bears made to be hugged.

The nuns dressed the children in frills and starched sailor suits, but nothing could hide the anemia, the rickets, the weak eyes and backward minds of these little ones as they marched and sang the Christmas carols. They were bewildered by so much glory. This event opened the door into a sad world of which I had known nothing but from then on I brought frequently ice cream or candy to the Orphanage. It made a strange contrast to the exotic life of the Island.

One morning late in January the Commissioner of Hawaiian institutions called me by telephone.

"Your Christmas tree has stirred up a hornet's nest at the leper settlement. They have petitioned the Governor to permit you to visit them. No white person has been there for eleven years. If you and your husband will go, we'll put a plane at your disposal next Friday morning."

"Yes, I'll go," I replied without knowing how I felt about it. I couldn't picture in my mind what it would be like. It was our first airplane flight. The familiar things of earth had a fourth-dimensional aspect. The sun shining on the ocean made it resemble a bowl of curdled milk. The spray flying up from Spouting Horn appeared as a white chiffon scarf hung above the rocks. The fields of pineapples looked like geometrical theorems while the orchards appeared to be growing fruit upside down. We passed over the rich ranches of the Island of Molokai and on the far side of sheer, tall cliffs we began to descend. The leper colony lies like an apron at the foot of a rocky precipice. On a barren point of land the plane came to rest and the pilot lent me his hand and I found myself standing on the loneliest spot in the wide world. The sand was of pulverized lava and black. The shallow water along the beach was also black. The waves did not dance in the sunshine but broke on the bleak shore as if they, too, knew only sadness. There were no little boats or craft of any kind anchored here, there was nothing that made a span of pleasure between land and sea. Instead the shore was sown with wooden crosses, row upon row — not upright but falling at different angles as though there was no one to straighten them. A striped black and white lighthouse rose stark and naked from the rocks. The picture was heartbreaking. Dear God, I thought, how will we live through a whole day on these forgotten reaches. No one met us. The pilot drove an ancient car over a mile of sunken land that lay between the lighthouse and the Colony and we drew up at a neat white cottage. In the doorway stood the Doctor. He greeted us warmly and had such a contented smile that involuntarily we inquired how long he had been here.

"About eleven years — my wife and I are happy — this must seem strange to you."

I was on the back seat of the motor and leaned forward to be sure I heard aright. Eleven years of voluntary exile!

"Before we go through the Colony, I want to explain our menage. The patients occupy the little houses around the square that confronts us as long as they can care for themselves; when the disease advances to the point where they can no longer do so, they are taken to one of our hospitals. We have three; one for men, one for women and one for the blind. While the lepers are able to keep house they buy their own provisions like other folks, the government gives a certain credit. Sometimes we have bargains and then there is a mad stampede for the marked down goods. They put up jams and jellies and pickles. We do everything possible to help them to lead normal lives. The process of disintegration varies greatly. We have had cases able to keep house eight or ten years, others reach the hospital within a few months. There is no way of telling.

"Letters come to us from all parts of the world, asking questions about the disease. We have to answer that we know very little — we are not even sure that it is contagious. Its origin is obscure — lack of food, unclean environment foster it. Immorality is not a cause direct, or indirect. The white man is more immune than other races, but occasionally even he contracts it in some mysterious way. Today we have no cure but in this age of science when miraculous drugs are being discovered, surely a panacea will come our way.

"I want Timothy to be the first to welcome you. He is one of the few educated white men ever brought here. He went through High School with no sign of the disease but the second year of college it was unmistakable and though he begged not to come here — what could the authorities do! He described his feelings when the plane set him down on the shore — there would never be a return to the life he had known — he was forever barred from the joys and struggles of the common man. The river Styx carrying the lost souls was his portion. His misery haunted me for days. But he is happy now as you will see. He is a great pet of my wife's; she lends him books and brings flowers to the shop where he works. Wait till you see the neat efficiency evident everywhere, though how he does it without fingers I don't know."

Timothy met us at his shop and we beheld the miracle

shelves where packages of oatmeal and cornstarch were stacked as straight as a die. We asked what authors he liked and promised to send him books and magazines. It was evident he had accepted his fate and had found immunity within. I could see that the Doctor loved him. We praised the shop and smiled a farewell since we couldn't shake hands.

"We have a Mormon Missionary here, I want you to meet him." We drove along the road until we came to a bearded man in a brown habit that made him look like a monk in a picture book.

"What are you doing?" we asked eagerly.

"Oh, I'm building a small jail just to make these folks feel they are human and nothing is as human as sin, the poets tell us. I came to the settlement because I thought a pair of hands would be useful and I guess they are, eh Doctor?"

"I don't know how we got along before you came, you're a godsend and no mistake." Turning to us the Doctor added, "When he's not working he's making us laugh or giving us a pep talk on how to dig trenches."

My husband was on the front seat and I leaned forward to get his reaction; the lugubrious atmosphere we had expected was nowhere in sight. We began to understand the spirit of sacrifice that pervaded this lost land.

The Doctor put on the brakes, sat back and lighted his pipe. It was evident that he had something of importance to impart.

"I am going to bring you to see Annie — she is our Jean d'Arc. But I want you to hear her story first. There are only a few cast iron rules for the institution and number one is no well person may accompany a leper and live in the Colony. But should a man or woman insist, the penalty is remaining the rest of their lives, whether the person who is a patient lives or dies. Not knowing whether the disease is contagious or not, we cannot take the chance of sending someone out to mingle with the populace. Annie signed away her freedom and remained with the husband she loved. For eight years they kept house and he seemed happy and scarcely to miss his old life and companions. Then Charles died and Annie had to face the prospect of the rest of her life among the lepers.

Annie came running down the steps of the hospital for the blind where every morning she read aloud. "My, but it's good to see folk from the big world, it's a real holiday for the Island." Turning her brown eyes on us, she exclaimed: "You can't imagine what a treat this is for us!"

"I want you to tell our visitors, Annie, what you have done to keep us old fogies up-to-date."

"Well, for a long time after Charles' death I wondered what I could do here for the rest of my life. My mind ran on the things I couldn't do — Heavens knows there were plenty of them! An inspiration was needed and every night I prayed that I might find one. All of a sudden an idea popped into my head — what if we could have movies! What if we could see the world of the living, the world we have lost. Once the notion lodged in my brain it gave me no rest. Not having the disease I could handle the films with immunity. How could we bring them over the cliffs of Molokai. It would take a goat to climb that precipice! A goat! That's what was needed! I asked the Commissioner to bring me a baby kid. One day he arrived with the baby wrapped in a piece of sail cloth and I set to work to train him. For one whole year he went half way up, turned and came bounding down again. I coaxed, I scolded, I beat him but all to no avail. One happy day he jumped beyond the rock where he could turn and was forced to go up all the way. Our friends in the administration were watching him from the topmost cliff and had ready a bountiful feast. A film was strapped round his middle and down he came like a hero from the wars. Now he goes flying up, leaping the crags that separate him from the banquet he knows awaits him.

"Twice a week we live in the great world; a world we cannot visit but that comes to us. We see how the women of fashion are dressed and the strange ornaments on women's hats. We shiver at sight of the tall buildings of New York and gasp at the gardens of Hollywood. Romance crosses the water as well as the mysteries of crime. We see soldiers marching and children — we love children."

We gazed at the woman who had exchanged freedom for love, a woman who, singlehanded, had dispelled isolation and brought the wide world to the black sands of Molokai. She was not to be pitied, a heroine who had created an epic and stood before us as a symbol of triumphant overcoming!

The Doctor pointed to a low building along the shore; "There's our theatre, it was a ramshackle old building that was no longed used. The Mormon, with what help we gave him, patched it up and donated a whole tin of paint to brighten its sides. We made seats out of an old boat, added empty kegs and there she was!"

The Doctor turned into a short lane; "I'm in the dress business — it's a side line but more successful than medicine, though I don't tell the Doctors that. It came about in this way: the women wear the striped institutional dresses and they hate them. When they go to church or the movies they can't dress up. I have a friend in the dry goods business and he sends me his unsold dresses at the end of each season. As the patients are without money, they pay in work — one hour for cotton, two for flounces and even longer for a dress with bow-knots!"

There in the window were the banners of coquetry flaunting their frills and gay colors. Even here Eve is tempted.

It was time for me to visit the women's hospital so the Doctor carried off my husband for a smoke and left me at the entrance of the Convent to await the nun who was to accompany me. I waited with a light heart, assimilating the values so suddenly thrust upon my consciousness. I reflected on the little dresses, with their frills bought with labor, with the desperate effort being made by a few that life should become bearable, with the sacrifice like a garment of protection thrown around their shoulders and the fragments of human nature strewn like pieces of wreckage by the sands of Molokai.

I was startled from my reflections by a vision in the doorway. It was a young woman, dressed in the habit and coif of the order, a costume designed to reduce young and old to a common denominator, but nothing could hide the flawless features, the shell pink skin, the deep blue eyes and the dimples. I blurted out my thoughts:

"What brings you here in your youth to bury yourself in this abode of sorrow?"

She looked past me and the dimples disappeared. "Because the knowledge came to me that on the other side of sacrifice lies happiness." She smiled and the dimples came back.

"I am Sister Cecille and am in charge of the hospital. Before we go into the wards I want to tell you what to expect. My unfortunates have begged to see you because you have befriended their children, but many are terrible to look upon. If fear or repulsion appears on your face, their cross will be the heavier because of your coming. Will you be able to hide your feelings? It is not easy, especially as we can have no rehearsal. There will be just this once to make it a failure or a success."

It was a serious moment and I wasn't sure I could control the situation. Looking into the nun's serene face I took courage; "Well, if you can give your whole life to this sacrifice, certainly I ought to be able to contribute one hour of mine."

We went in. The angels must have stood beside us, for unaided I should have sunk to the floor and covered my eyes. The women were in the last stages of the disease, their flesh melting from their bones. They crowded around me, they pressed against me, eager for news of their children. They searched my face for the answers to their unspoken questions. We stood, the nun, the dying, and I, making a compact whole. The first plunge was appalling, but afterwards I knew I had shown no fear and this conquest made the visit what the nun had hoped for, and as we came out into the sunshine Sister Cecille squeezed my arm, saying:

"It was a miracle from our Lord."

I bade an affectionate farewell to the lovely saint who had given me a glimpse of her halo through sacrifice, a glimpse I was never to lose.

The Doctor's wife drove me back to her cottage. As we drank our tea she spoke of her own reactions to life in the Colony.

"When we first came I thought I should die! My husband had waited years for a chance to investigate leprosy, so I knew here we would stay. I gritted my teeth and began a garden; first a vegetable garden and afterwards flowers. When there was no more land to spade up I bought paint in Honolulu and gave the house a coat inside and out. We went that Summer on a vacation and when I put the key in the lock of our front door I knew this was my home.

"I believe I understand your part in the heaped-up sacrifices of the Island."

Here, indeed, was the indomitable spirit of man. That spirit that led Father Damien to lay down his life among the lepers; that brought Brother Ambroise to unfurl his flag on these shores; that compelled Mother Julianna and her nuns to move in a never-ending procession of mercy.

Among the lasting values of life is the impetus that makes us lift our brother when he falls, thus do we weave the Golden Rule into the fabric of our lives. We need the sparkle, the gaiety of ephemeral delights but they do not build the eternal verities.

We did not utter a word on the homeward flight.

Though in after years we visited many lands and found much to admire in each, yet ever since, in looking back upon that memorable day, we have believed that if there is a spot where Heaven bends down and touches earth, it is on the black sands of Molokai, here in the Leper Colony.

Chapter 17

I EXPLORE CAMBRIDGE AND LONDON

The National Spiritual Assembly asked me, while in England, to negotiate for the purchase of Prof. E. G. Browne's *Traveller's Narrative*. From the catalogue of the Cambridge Press for 1929 they learned it was in the market. So as soon as I reached London I dispatched a letter to the President of the Cambridge Press, asking for an interview. His prompt response was an invitation to come to Cambridge and I set off for the famous university that had been a going concern since the Twelfth Century. I mounted the magnificent flight of steps in a state of trepidation, not familiar with the formalities the meeting involved. The rooms on either side of the main hall were lined with cedar presses, carefully labeled, but before I could make a proper tour of inspection, the door opened and British Culture in the flesh stood before me. I don't remember his name, a fact that goes to show how careless one is in lining the shelves of memory, retaining information of a non-essential character and recalling useless things. Now I recall his shoes, the cloth tops, the pointed toes, having no bearing on the interview. He proceeded to initiate me into the history of printing and the important part Cambridge played in the cultural growth of England. I managed to wedge in one question — had he known Prof. Browne well? "Oh yes, I knew him well, one of the most brilliant minds of our day. Towards the end of his life his judgment was warped due to the disease that caused his death. A pity," he added sadly, "that such a great mind should have been wasted over the study of an ambiguous and unimportant Oriental cult."

I could not resist the retort that the fame of Prof. Browne, nay, that of Cambridge University itself, would rest in the future on the fact that the Bahá'í religion had been first investigated and brought before the Occidental public by one of the faculty of this institution. He dismissed the opinion of a crude American, by a polite wave of his well-shaped hand and proceeded, by an alternate route, to the subject of the vaults that store the published books. "These vaults," he said, "are specially constructed so that they are fire-proof, burglar-proof; they have been made secure from the assaults of earth and heaven and yet" (here he paused) "from the vaults the plates of this particular volume are missing! The disappearance is unique in the annals of printing. Since the inception of the University such a thing has never occurred before. How it happened no one knows! A book published and without proper plates cannot be retained." I was seeking a moment in which to introduce the matter of price, since that was what I had come for, but it was difficult in this rarified atmosphere to formulate the question on this errant volume. Finally I said, "How much money will it involve?" He looked startled, nonplussed at the word money, so crude, so American! However, he preserved his dignity and replied coldly: "We are not selling the book – without proper plates it is useless to us – our agent, I have been informed, mentioned one hundred dollars to cover packing and insuring."

How strange are the ways of Providence! How subtle the devices by which men are forced to relinquish age-long traditions in the Day of God! I returned to London with a signed receipt in my pocket for a book no money could buy – no robber could steal! A volume that henceforth and forever belonged to the Bahá'ís.

The stronghold of culture in Cambridge University having been successfully breached, I began to haunt the Museums of London for a trace of Bahá'u'lláh's Tablet to Queen Victoria. I found in the person of the Curator of the British Museum a wingless angel who took my quest right to his heart. He led me, at once, to a case containing a Tablet of 'Abdu'l-Bahá, written on creamy vellum in gold ink, a delicate tracery in pale blue framing its two pages. It was inscribed to a Persian living in London some years ago and had with it no translation. When nothing further eventuated, the Curator wrote a letter to the Master of Manuscripts at Windsor and packed me off. He promised to seek in the locked cabinets of the Museum while I was absent for Bahá'í treasures.

I went to Windsor, where I was relayed from one Castle official to another until finally I learned that the Curator had gone to London for a few hours and was expected in the early afternoon. I spent a charming morning rambling amid splendors of the past, sniffing the rarified air of vanished glories. The Curator returned. He read the letter and ordered china tea and watercress sandwiches and under an arbor of roses, during this delicate repast, he told me what he surmised had happened to the Oriental treasures given Queen Victoria. Numberless presents and letters had arrived from Oriental Potentates and to preserve these Victoria had ordered cedar chests made, ornamented by iron scroll work and finished by medieval locks. When Edward the VII came to the throne, he had the caskets transported to Balmoral Castle in Scotland. Whether any further change had been made since the World War he did not know. Alas, I was unable to go to Scotland and follow up his surmise. At least there was one probability to remember. On Monday morning, I returned to the British Museum. Perhaps no one approaching that formidable building — with its Ionic facade; its circular reading room of one hundred and forty feet where three hundred readers can be accommodated; its dome of one hundred and six feet; its great quadrangle — would dream of applying "homelike" as a descriptive adjective of it; yet the effect of one person's kindness and interest was that it actually created this warm illusion as I entered and knocked on the door of the Curator's private office. He answered the knock and with a beaming smile said, "Come, I have found something important."

He led me down the corridor and turned to a small door
that he unlocked by a mighty key hanging alone on a wire
ring. He closed and locked the door behind us and, opening
a cabinet, laid on the table "The Star Tablet" of the Báb. I
knew I could not have the original; I dared not even touch the
paper across whose surface the Báb's hand had rested. We
were both silent and then I asked if it could be photographed
and could I have the replica? "Yes, with proper witnesses this
can be done."

The Museum's photographer was summoned. His preparations for the event were almost as elaborate as for a corona-
tion in Westminster Abbey. During the hours I waited I did
sigh for a fast-working, agile American! The photographer
appeared, he then disappeared for long stretches of time, he
then reappeared, adjusted the machine and disappeared again.
After four hours of suspense I limped back to the Grovenor
Hotel clutching the precious replica. I wrote Shoghi Effendi
at once, sending him the picture and he replied that it was
necessary to send it to Persia to make sure of its genuineness
as many manuscripts had been copied by the followers of
Yahyá, an enemy of the Faith. I heard nothing more. I knew
the process would take time. But in 1944, as the Centennial
committee made their final rounds before the opening of the
National Convention in the Bahá'í Temple at Wilmette, we
walked through the Foundation Hall to gaze at the treasures
accorded us by the Guardian. On the center wall I caught
sight of "The Star Tablet," beautifully framed. It was the true
Tablet from the Báb! The sight of it filled me with happiness!
How much I owe the Curator who had at great pains and
search secured for us this priceless jewel.

Chapter 18

IN THE VALLEY OF SHADOWS

One morning in November, 1929, I was seized with a strange pain in my chest and threw myself on the bed. From that casual siesta I did not lift my head again until February was waning. Rapidly I developed pneumonia — the fatal type three. No serum had been discovered to quell its poison. Every breath I drew was a struggle with a never-ending strangulation. My head in an oxygen tent, time ticked away in agony. Many nights Dr. Wheelwright, our physician, spent at the bedside, doctors were called in consultation but daily the disease mounted and my resistance weakened. It was evident nothing more could be done and it was announced to the family that I must succumb. My daughter, Wanden, on hearing this dire verdict, cabled the Guardian for prayers. The Guardian replied that "your mother's work is not finished and she will live to complete it." In March, I opened my eyes on a world familiar yet strange. I could breathe again and without agony but I could not move. I could not even turn my head. An overpowering weakness had spread through my body. Dr. Wheelwright, who before had not believed in miracles, saw one now with his own eyes. He did not understand that Shoghi Effendi's prayers had returned life, but he repeatedly said that nothing in his medical career had prepared him for my recovery. Very gently he told me I could no longer live by the sea. No more New York, no more Italy, I must make a home in the Rocky Mountains of Colorado. It was probable, he said, that I might never speak out loud again. But he had not read 'Abdu'l-Bahá's letter saying, I "should roar

across the seven seas." Destiny is a thing apart from knowledge, it is a dimension not in books but descends upon us, in
the measure that the Supreme Being wills, and no man know-
eth.

Like Swiss Family Robinson the moving began, the heir-
looms, the books, the furniture and the kitchen pans were
packed and shipped to Colorado Springs, the unknown locale
of our future life.

When I could maintain an upright position and take a few
steps we entrained for the West. On a starry night we looked
out and there was the Mississippi flowing by, that mighty river
that divides and again unites the land; the train was carrying
us over the dark waters into the archway of the West. Colorado
Springs received us coldly. It was snowing, it was bleak and
desolate, low clouds obscured the mountains and for the first
days I felt more as though I had a prison sentence than life
renewed. But the potency of Colorado air, that high dry alti-
tude that fills the body with health, soon brought an incredible
change. An all-pervading energy began to filter through me
and bring my being back to activity.

As the high points of sight-seeing were unknown, we acqui-
esced to whatever plan the chauffeur suggested and it was
quite by accident that one bright afternoon he drove out to
Pine Valley. It is a small level space enclosed by low mesas
and locked at the far end by mountains. It is in no way spectacular, nor is it more beautiful than many other valleys but
it brought a quickening of the heart; it had a dreamlike quality
that one feels only when returning to the scenes of one's chil-
hood. I felt that I was unlocking a door of which I had held
the key all my life. We bought a few acres and, not feeling
certain that this would be a permanent abode, decided to
send East for a portable house. It arrived in neat sections,
the front door already had a knocker; shutters were attached
to the windows, the whole affair was like a stage set and was
put together and in place in a week! There was a roof above,
floors under the feet, doors that opened and shut and closets

with hooks. We walked in and sat down in our house! But we were novices, amateurs, the natives shook their heads; "It will never stand more than one winter," they declared. We were reckoning without the winter gales and storms that blew the rocks out of the ground. "You will find a heap of ruins," quoth the wise, "when you return in the spring. This is a make-believe thing, not an honest-to-God dwelling suitable for man and beast." Well, there we were! It was up! It was paid for! Why had we not inquired; none of these reflections solved the problem. We consulted our wise Roy and he conferred with two bricklayers — they could help, he said, if anyone could. We sat down and looked up at the abode so jauntily perched on the hillside. First let us read over the instructions sent with the portable house. We did, and found that no weight of any kind could be placed on the structure. About these challenging enigmas, we came to a decision. It was to enclose the house with brick, a quarter of an inch from the clapboards, placing the bricks on a foundation of their own and cementing them to the main building. "Very practical," agreed the three men, and they set to work.

Each day the brick spread over the boards and rose higher. Heavy wrought iron columns were added to the support of the roof. Soon a solid expanse of brick and iron opposed the elements. The winds and storms of the future held no terrors for "Temerity," a name we had given the place to indicate the courage it took to become citizens of the wilds.

Part Three
I Commence My Travels

Chapter 19

MARTHA ROOT

Restored to health, I wrote the Guardian asking if there was any special country he would like me to visit. He replied that it was of utmost importance to visit Central and South America. No one had been there since Martha Root's journey in 1919. Our contemporaries did not regard these countries as being in the orbit of travel so at first my husband considered the project doubtful but once he settled down with the maps and schedules the prospect brightened. I determined to see Martha Root for I felt the value of the voyage depended upon having her advice.

The moment I arrived in New York I drove through wind and rain to the Martha Washington Hotel where I found her in a cubicle — it couldn't be termed a room. Martha was surrounded by small bags and bundles in preparation for her coming trip to Europe. How calm she was! I felt like a small tug beside an ocean liner — would I ever attain such magnificent poise! She gave a picture of how the idea of going to South America came to her. She had a sum of money left her by her father and in prayer she constantly saw herself in this far land. So persistent was the vision that she wrote 'Abdu'l-Bahá and he answered, "Go thou to South America." She set off on July 22 which is midwinter in the land below us.

We had at the time one tiny pamphlet in Spanish, and armed with the Mighty Word she visited many of the cities of Latin America. She described her journey, riding a mule, over the heights of the Andes with a company of other sojourners. They climbed the dizzy peaks and at the top passed

71

through a pitch black tunnel, frightening even the mules, who shied and slipped in the inky vault. The downward slopes were even more dangerous and they were obliged to dismount and walk along the edge of the precipice. All the time Martha was repeating the Greatest Name of God, calling down the blessings on this wild country. (The mountain pass over which Martha travelled was obliterated by a landslide shortly afterward and has not been reopened to date — 1951).

Martha expressed delight that I was going — gave me addresses and a crowning gift of the Tablet 'Abdu'l-Bahá had written for inquirers and sent to South America. (This Tablet is now in the National Bahá'í Archives at Wilmette). Taking my arm she walked with me to the elevator reminding me that *every* minute belongs to God, not every other minute. South America was Martha's initial step in her years of service to the Faith. At her death in Honolulu in 1939 the Guardian named her a "Hand of the Cause." She was the first American to fulfill this great station.

Chapter 20

TURNING SOUTH

We embarked on the *Santa Lucia* with Panama the first stop. Passing through the locks it was not of the engineers I thought but of the two Doctors who, believing that a certain type of mosquito caused yellow fever, offered to be bitten by these insects. Dr. Lazeard died and Dr. Carroll was an invalid for life, but their sacrifice made possible the building of the Panama Canal.

The city is fascinating and our ten days passed all too swiftly. The West coast of South America is arid due to the idiosyncrasies of the Humboldt Current and there is only one big city — Lima, Peru. Here the Inca civilization wiped out by the Spanish conquest followed in turn by the growth of a modern city augered well, I felt in my bones, for the establishment of the Faith, as it has since proved. Valparaiso was as cold as New York and we were glad for the shelter of a small modest hotel. We looked into conditions of the city with a view to the coming pioneers and drove, one windy day, to Vina del Mar with the spray flying over the roof tops. Though the distance between Valparaiso and Santiago is short, the sea might be hundreds of miles away. The city of Santiago is enclosed by towering mountains and the sunsets throw vivid colors across the icy slopes of the Andes. Blues and purples and streaks of pink cause the mountains to glow like immense rainbows. The clouds as they sail over the mountain tops are reflected as in a mirror. It is one of the great spectacular views of the world.

We went directly to the Y.W.C.A. and asked permission

73

to give a Bahá'í talk. Those in charge could not have been more cordial; they gave the invitations and arranged the details so when we arrived the next afternoon the room was filled. Present among the people were the directors of the Sweet Memorial Hospital and clinic, the personnel from the Y.M.C.A. of Valparaiso, the President of the college and four ministers. Mr. Mathews opened the meeting by reading a quotation from *The Promulgation of Universal Peace,* that begins "The Divine Manifestations since the day of Adam have striven to unite humanity so that all men would be accounted as one soul." When he closed the book, one of the ministers asked him to read the passage again. This happy and unexpected request was the keynote of the afternoon. I spoke on "Widening our Horizons" and the talk was followed by a friendly discussion and many questions. It was dark when we stepped into the street. We had discovered an inconspicuous restaurant where the chef served a ragout of chicken, rice, slices of egg and onion, topped with whipped potatoes well browned. We brought home this recipe and it became a great favorite at the International School, where it was dubbed "The Chilian Dish."

A Mr. Stone from Cook's Travel Bureau had been in the audience at the Y. His command of Spanish was perfect and together we planned that he should read a chapter from *Bahá'u'lláh and the New Era* at a literary society that he had formed. During the five months before he was transferred to São Paulo he faithfully followed this program. As Martha Root did not teach in Santiago, I believe my Bahá'í address was the first to be given there. Frances Stewart was among the early teachers sent to Chili. Her lectures were highly regarded by the government officials, as was proved by her being asked to broadcast, both to Europe and America, the news of the disastrous earthquake that occurred in the city of Concepción.

Chapter 21

THE LAKES OF CHILI

We had been looking at the Andes through the colored lens of Santiago for many days and we knew the time had come to continue our journey. The question was, how should we go? Martha had travelled over the high mountain passes and we felt impelled to choose another route. After considerable debate we decided to risk crossing the Lakes, though winter winds were rising and ominous chill from the Antarctic was creeping over the land. The start of our trip seemed propitious and the trials ahead were veiled from our eyes. A train ran as far as Osorno and alighting at that station we found an ancient taxi. Would the man drive us to Ensenada? He shrugged his shoulders — spread out his hands in a despairing gesture and having given us fair warning, proceeded to crank up the car. There was no road, only ruts that ran between fields of lava and lava is not a substance to tread upon lightly. The car skidded, bounded forward, rolled backward and swerved in a continuous motion during the four and a half hours of seasick waverings. At last the welcome lights of Ensenada on Lake Llanquihue appeared and heaven could not have looked more blessed! There was only a single cabin by the shore, amid a sea of dripping leaves. This cabin served as an inn and we were ushered into a sliver of a room, austere as a Trappist cell. The beds were made of logs, without pillows, linen or mattresses — only red wool blankets; there was no furniture, only a tin basin and pitcher. Mr. Mathews, a fiend for fresh air, attempted to open the window, but it was securely nailed against the damp world without. "Did Shoghi Effendi

75

say we had to come here?" exclaimed Matt angrily. "No, he left all our plans to us believing we had common sense and were grown up." "Oh," said Matt and beat a hasty retreat. When I entered the sitting room I found him talking German with our host, sampling his most excellent cheese and in the best of humor.

At the Inn there was only one other couple, a Senor and Senora de Burmuilt who came to audit the books at the end of the season. When the Senora could no longer restrain her curiosity, she asked why I was at this outpost of civilization and where I was bound. Eagerly I gave my reason. Because a Prophet had come to the earth with a New Message and it was necessary to spread the news to every individual, we must tell the story. She listened with deep attention and after a thoughtful pause said: "My dear lady, everything in this world must have a head — the Catholic Church has a Pope, the English Church has an Archbishop, each country has a ruler — it is a law — have you then in your religion such a leader?"

"Yes," I replied, "we have a Guardian appointed and bequeathed to us by the Interpreter of the Prophet." She looked at me keenly and leaning over addressed her husband, "Listen Gustave, did you know the world has a Guardian — one who is destined to guide mankind and bring about a New Order?"

"Thank God for that — how else shall we be delivered from the chaos and despair of the present day — a Guardian is the only one who can direct us." He drew his chair over to mine and began asking searching questions, fundamental questions inherent in the German mind. The terms used — what do they mean? The word Báb, explain it. "It means 'The Gate'," I answered, "and his coming was foretold by Daniel. The Báb proclaimed his own station in these wonderful words: 'I am the Mystic Fane that the hand of the Almighty hath reared.'" He wrote this down on the back of an envelope. "And what is the meaning of the title Bahá'u'lláh?" "It means 'The Glory of God.'" His face lighted; there was something in that Name that seemed to awaken his whole being.

Far into the night we talked and they told me something of their own lives. After World War I they decided to leave Germany and settle where their children would be removed from war and hate. They came to Chili and took a small house in Porto Varas. Many of their neighbors were German and they had a club called "Study of Liberal Thought." They felt confident that this group would follow them into the Bahá'í Faith. Among my pamphlets was Shoghi Effendi's *Goal of the New World Order*. I gave it to them and, fired by enthusiasm for this wonderful treatise, Senora began translating it into Spanish in long hand. It took many hours but at last it was finished and it was, except the early pamphlet, the first translation of the Bahá'í writings into Spanish. For six years this devoted couple labored for the Faith, pioneering among their friends. But in 1939 Hitler reached across the seas and took away their two sons and the next year sent for their daughter. Finally, I received a note written in an alien hand, telling me they were in danger, their mail was opened and that it would be wiser for me not to write. I never heard again. But they came in the early dawn of Bahá'í history in South America — they accepted the Faith after sifting it to the core. They were the first to translate the Words and their memory belongs in the annals of the early pioneers.

The next morning my husband ransacked the Inn for a schedule of the steamers crossing Lake Llanquihue. Finding none, he appealed to the Innkeeper. "The steamer goes out," was his philosophical reply, "when it takes a notion to come in, like a coot when he's through hiding — I have known the time when she appeared twice a week but lately once has been our quota. Mighty blasts warn us of her arrival and down we scurry to the wharf." A few more precious days the de Burmuilts and I had to speak about the Faith and to read together. Then one morning the silence was shattered by three violent blasts and in a moment the Inn was in turmoil! Boarding an ocean liner was mild in comparison. Sr. and Sra. de Burmuilt insisted on accompanying us and Sra. de Burmuilt and I sat on the front seat with the driver and our husbands in the rear. Ahead I noticed a waterfall and wondered how we were going to avoid it, when suddenly the driver put on speed and the cascade poured over us. We tumbled out, shook the water from our clothes, dried off the seats and spread a fresh towel over. Laughing and pretending to make light of the incident we climbed back on the seats and I thought, well — that's that! But what was my horror at a bend in the road to spy another cataract more alarming than the first. The chauffeur stepped on the accelerator and we dived under — this time nothing was said nor did we dismount. Dripping, we survived still another torrent that fell from the rocks above. The sacrifice the de Burmuilts were making to see us off included the wetting from six separate waterfalls, three each way!

We boarded the sturdy boat of tarred planks; puffing steam and sending waves of spray, she backed into deep water. Our friends stood on the bank, waving and calling blessings upon our voyage. As their figures grew dim my heart was heavy, to find friends in the Faith and lose them so soon. I envy the cat with his nine lives — one life is hardly long enough to contain the recollections, emotions and changes with which it is crowded; they are cramped into a corner of the mind, instead of having room to hold their true proportions.

The Lake of All Saints (its English translation) was a prototype of all the lakes through which we passed. Trees crowded the shores and dipped their leaves in the water — there was no human habitation — there was no sound save the lapping water — there was the trackless shore, above the unconquered mountains of ice that sent a thousand cascades tumbling into the lakes from the glaciers, the downpour of light seemed to flow like a living stream. The picture before one might have been entitled "Creation." Each day the wind grew wilder, the shores took on wintry colors and now we came to the last of the chain of lakes, Nahuel Huipi. It is the longest and at its head lies Bariloche, like a jewel of green enamel. Crossing this lake was dreadful — the little steamer shuddered under the impact of wind and waves. We hugged the shore, endeavoring to avoid the worst of the elements. Every part of the boat was covered with spray and we gave up trying to dodge the water that continually poured over us. We sat resigned, indifferent to discomfort, praying only for land. When the lights of Bariloche were seen twinkling through the mist a shout of joy went up from the passengers. I can never forget the kindness I received from the landlady of the Inn, who put me to bed and plied me with hot drinks and wooly blankets to dispel the chills.

One train a week ran between Buenos Aires and Bariloche. It came in on Wednesday and departed on Sunday and was a center of social gaiety. Women in bright shawls and skirts came from the outlying districts, their arms full of flowers, to decorate the interior of the train. Children clambered over the engine, polishing the already shining chrome and brass. On Sunday the station platform assumed the air of a fiesta. Brightness was everywhere and though we knew no one, we had an affectionate send-off! The women waved, the children blew kisses, and the band played, and the long journey of two and a half days was begun in a frolicsome spirit. On the train we met the Lavorellos, mother and two daughters, who initiated us into the national drink, mate tea. The girls, curious as to my errand of religious announcement, became interested up to a point, but not far enough to withstand family and social prestige. The pampas of moving grain flowed by mile after mile, often growing so high that the cattle were lost to view. Sometimes we came upon heaps of burning grain — there was more than could be used or sold. Thus we passed through the greatest grazing country in the world, into the Capitol of the Argentine, Buenos Aires.

Chapter 22

THE ARGENTINE

It was raining in Buenos Aires. I risked the downpour to present the letters of introduction that I had brought. My expedition was fruitless. No one was in town. I did not know what to do next realizing that there wasn't a single human being in this great city to whom I could appeal. I fell back upon the power of prayer. I believed that I had relied on prayer before but in looking back I saw that I had cherished other means of attaining my desires — there were other loyalties that could be marshalled to my aid. It was my first experience in absolute reliance upon prayer. It seemed strange that I had to journey all the way to South America to discover a simple spiritual law, but so it was! I no longer heard the rain. I walled my mind against all other thought and prayed with all my might that God would not allow me to leave the Argentine until I had given the Message of Bahá'u'lláh.

The rain continued to beat against the window-panes and I continued to bombard the portals of Heaven. The second day I had a feeling that an answer hovered near. When prayer is answered it is not in meager measure — not by a tithe of good fortune, but by the outpouring of blessings as from a cornucopia. In the opulence of its nature, it outstrips all forms of generosity. In the evening of the second day a large envelope was pushed under my door. It was a request from the American Women's Club to give a talk on the Modern Drama! This was my "open sesame" and I replied in the affirmative. Fortunately while in New York I had seen three provocative plays and on this scant thread I strung a discourse. Next

81

morning the daily press announced that a dramatic critic was
in town — I had to back away from so false an introduction
and persuaded my husband to invite the reporters to lunch.
I assured them that I had something far more important to
bring them than was contained in the world of make-believe.
"Well," they chorused. "Go right ahead, tell us about it." "It
is called Bahá'í."

The poised pencils came down on the table. "Oh, come
now, something simple please, we can't go into Oriental
terms." "Let me explain: this word means followers of the
light or glory. Just one word that will be used the world
around, no translations into German, Spanish, French or in
any other language, so you see it is quite simple, after all. The
thing you must do, is to help me to familiarize the word
'Bahá'í' to the public." The pencils came down on the blank
page. "How is it spelled?" "B A H Á ' Í!" They wrote it down.
"Tell us about it but make it brief, we only have thirty minutes
at noon."

The next day the *Daily Standard* published on the editorial
page one of the most comprehensive articles ever to appear
from the press. I called Mr. Timmins to thank him. "I should
like to come up and get another scoop on this new religion."
So he came and we talked and I asked him to use the name
several times in succession. So, instead of one editorial we
had four and the word "Bahá'í" appeared successively and its
reasons for being amplified.

Chapter 23

THE COUNTESS STORY

Among the invitations I had to speak was one asking me to address a Spanish Business Girls' Club. None of the girls spoke English so I had to look about for an interpreter. One who had studied English in the States was recommended to me by the Y.W.C.A. and I found her glad to have the practice. How often I thought of 'Abdu'l-Bahá who had submitted to this trial over a period of years. One does not know how close to the original the interpreter is following, nor how one's meaning is being phrased. When I made a short statement and paused, my companion contrived a flowing speech of considerable length; whereas when I explained a point more fully, she followed with a few staccato sentences. The girls belonging to the club were young, there was only one exception in the audience, an elderly woman who sat far back in the corner. She was dressed after the fashion of a Spanish Grandee and as the talk progressed seemed more and more agitated. When the ordeal was over, the old lady beckoned me and asked me very earnestly to call on her the next morning. She put into my hand a card on which was engraved "Countessa Helena Marie de Barrill."

The house I sought occupied a whole block. I had noticed it and from its size had imagined it to be a public building. The entrance was hard to come by, as the gate formed part of a high iron fence tipped with gold spikes. When I found my way to the front door I was ushered into a small reception room, the walls covered by Louis XV tapestry, every article breathed luxury and spoke of the old world. The Countessa opened the door, came forward and embraced me; seating herself on the opposite side of a small table she poured out the story she had waited so many years to tell.

"I was born," she began in a low voice, "in Madrid, Spain, as was my husband also. While we were still young, Alphonse was asked to come to the Argentine and open the First National Bank of Spain. This was a great opportunity for a young man and so we came to Buenos Aires and made it our home. We prospered, and if you have visited the Cathedral you may have remarked about the stained-glass windows that we had designed by the great artist D'albe in Spain. They were transported one by one." I made a deprecatory motion and she resumed her story. "Being Catholic we brought up our children under the advice of the Archbishop, a pious and worthy man. We took no step without consulting him. Thus did our lives flow by in happiness and comfort. We were unaware of the passage of time. I had never considered an end to our happy life and union, so you may imagine my horror and astonishment when our family physician took me aside and disclosed to me that my husband had an incurable malady. I struggled with all my might against such a doom. I rang up the Cathedral and had more Masses said; I called in eminent physicians in consultation; I changed nurses frantically but to no avail. Day by day he grew weaker until I was not even sure that he recognized me. We had by this time a resident doctor and one fatal day he advised me to stay with him quietly for the end was not far off. I opened the door of my husband's chamber and went in. The room had been darkened and seemed strange and foreign — suddenly I felt afraid, I knew not of what. With trepidation I approached the bed and took one of his hands. He opened his eyes and gazed at me for a long moment and then spoke. His voice seemed to come from a great distance. 'Marie, there is something wonderful on this earth that we know nothing about — it is called BAHÁ'Í — when I am here no more — go seek it — it is.'

"He broke off, closed his eyes and spoke no more. I stood

rooted to the spot and do not know how long it was until someone came and led me away. What did this mysterious word mean? How was I to find out? I pondered these questions in my heart but spoke of it to no one. A few months passed and then I packed my bare necessities and with my faithful Anna set out upon the strange quest. Far and wide we travelled and everywhere I asked, 'Do you know where I can find Bahá'í?' The people shook their heads — they did not know whither to direct me. Only then did I realize that I had never made a decision in my whole life. When I was young my parents decided everything, and later it was my husband or the Archbishop who took over my management. A child of ten could not have been more bewildered by the big world than was I. I lingered in some town or city because I had no idea where to go next, indeed, had it not been for Anna's strong will, I should never have reached home. Often in the night awaking, I wondered had I mistaken the words my husband spoke and yet, in my mind persisted that word 'Bahá'í.' Thus nine years passed in disappointment and confusion. Nine years! Then you came and again, I heard the word that had been ringing in my mind like a bell. A word that seemed to echo from the other world and fall into my soul. Last night I prayed in thankfulness that there was yet time to fulfill the dying command of Alphonse. Can you imagine what this means to me?" The emotional tension was so great I could only press her hands and wipe the tears from my eyes. Reflecting on this remarkable event I can only conjecture that this soul in passing from one plane to another, had, for a flash, envisioned both the earthly and eternal planes. Surely a rare phenomenon!

The lessons I gave Marie differed from all others. She drank in the Revelation as a thirsty pilgrim in the desert might drink at a spring. She shed her years and became joyous and animated. Often she would clap her hands like a child and cry out, "Oh, how wonderful that is." Everything connected with the Bahá'í Message filled her with delight. There were no arguments — there was none of the fear of losing Christ so often felt in teaching Christians. She perceived that what we taught was added to the words of Jesus, and that only man-made dogmas were forgotten. Here was a soul filled by the light of a Divine Revelation, seeing it in its true proportions.

The day dawned that was to carry us on another stage of our journey, this time to Brazil. The Prince line sailed from the mouth of the Platte River. The steamer tied to a worn and mangy wharf. What was my surprise to see the Countessa, aided by her aged coachman and still more feeble footman, carrying a heavy object on to the wharf. As I drew near to embark, these three old people unfurled a large standard made of white satin on which, embossed in gold and silver was a single word "Bahá'u'lláh."

Footnote: It had been agreed between us that in the spring the Countessa should go to Geneva in order to meet Lady Bloomfield. She set out on this voyage with her faithful Anna and arrived safely. She died in Switzerland not long after her arrival.

Chapter 24

BRAZIL

It is interesting to remember how little Portugal came into possession of this vast tract of land. When Pope Alexander VI was dividing the new territory, he had no map and supposing that beyond the mountains lay the sea, and having no idea of the nose of Brazil, he drew his pencil down the spur of the Andes and handed, all unwittingly, the major portion of the land to Portugal.

The beauty of Rio de Janeiro is spectacular; you seem to have stepped off the planet earth on to one unknown, which indeed, in many ways you have. A necklace of mountains pierces the cerulean sky while far below stretches a wide scalloped petticoat of white sand, lapped by the sea. Strange shades of green coast down the hills and are lost in the surf.

The surrounding loveliness paled before the joy of meeting the one and only Bahá'í on the continent of South America, Leonora Holsapple (now Mrs. Armstrong). She informed me that the law required that one who was to speak in public, must give a sample talk before the Guardians of Moral and Religious Training. They are chosen because they are strict Catholics, this being the religion of Brazil. When I recited my piece I wrapped myself in a bland and childlike aura and told little stories not calculated to awaken the sleeping brain. Though I believe they knew I was not telling ALL, which of course was the case, they gave me a grudging and uneasy permission, mainly because Krishna Murti was in town, drawing people after him like the Pied Piper, with the whole wharf covered with rose petals for his holy feet to press.

87

At the Bank of England I found Mr. Cecil Best to whom
I had a letter of introduction. He received me kindly and explained that he had a large following of Sufis. These appeared
to have no connection with the Persian Sufis but came from
India via England. He invited me to address them, an invitation that I gladly accepted. His house was high up in the hills,
directly opposite the great cross erected on the summit of
one of the mountains; the flying clouds below gave the effect
of a cross floating in the sky. Of Sufis large and small there
were about forty. I had a gracious introduction from Mr.
Best. The audience listened to the Message with rapt attention and when I finished they crowded around me to tell me
that it was exactly what they believed!

"Have you a Prophet whose words you follow?" I queried.
No, they had no Prophet yet the belief was a counterpart of
Bahá'í. I was fascinated and went three times to the hilltop to
discover what they did believe and how I could bring them to
the realization of the Faith. I never was able to gain the slightest idea of what it was all about. It was like a dream where
everything seems right and natural and yet means nothing! I
found Mr. and Mrs. Best a sincere and charming couple and
I believe had I been able to remain we might have coalesced;
I was hungry to bring that group of worthy people into the
Faith.

I learned a few words in Portuguese and, not wishing to
impose on Leonora's time, decided to go shopping on my own.
I had caught sight of a lovely crimson taffeta that I thought
would suit Temerity and wanted to examine it at close range.
I could not connect the words I knew together, and soon exhausted my vocabulary and bogged down in my efforts to
bargain. The shopkeeper waited for the right moment and
then said with a sardonic smile, "O.K. baby, I come from
Brooklyn and the price is just the same as if you were in Macy's
basement."

Leonora had advised us to visit Santos and São Paula and,
indeed, it was a rewarding trip. The business section of São

Paulo is very impressive. We visited the Snake Farm, an establishment that has reduced death from snake bites from eighty to thirty-five per cent. It is impossible to realize in North America the benefit of this unique and already famous scientific organization. That year coffee was too plentiful and around the wharves of Santos were great hills of chocolate colored beans going to waste. The storehouses advised by Bahá'u'lláh would have prevented such a tremendous loss.

I owe much to my experience in giving the Faith in Brazil for here I encountered a state of mind that broke up the fixed mold of my teaching. I realized that you must accommodate your words, clothe your expressions, in the terms of the land in which you are. The Latin people are not the prickly pears met with in the Northern countries but they must be appealed to with emotion, with spiritual insight, rather than with cold reason. They must be studied and understood before you can make a deep impression on their minds.

Chapter 25

YUCATÁN

From South America we took a boat to Yucatán via Cuba. At Havana we were obliged to transship, as Yucatán lies outside frequented steamship lines and only one boat a month touches there. The coast of Yucatán is inhospitable in the extreme; sandbars stretch far out to sea forcing steamers to anchor several miles from shore, while passengers must be brought in by means of small boats. Was it force of circumstances, adventure, or destiny that brought an ancient people to choose this land as the center of their religious and intellectual life that existed for more than a thousand years? The ruins, vast in extent as well as beauty, have educed sighs of admiration from the whole world, yet they are hidden like jewels in a mine.

The land, like the sea, is flat. Rivers run underground and give no sign of their existence save for a luxurious vegetation. Even while we sat on the wharf waiting for officials, the values of yesterday slipped away; waiting in the sunshine appeared a normal occupation and the hours elongated so that there was time left over. Every place has its tempo, staccato or slow, measured or quick, and thus you learn to keep step with each and be in tune with all.

Sometime in the afternoon we drove to Mérida, the only city of any considerable size in Yucatán. One can see how charmingly planned the city had been, with three rows of trees on each side of wide streets and plantings of flowers and shrubs in the center. Once it must have been an oasis of fragrant beauty in a parched land. Now its grandeur is bowed in the dust. Stately mansions copied from the French villas of the eighteenth century are loud in lamentation. Streaks of paint blacken the walls, oval windows are without panes, while lawns are littered with stucco roses and cupids that have fallen from ornate cornices. Whole blocks are boarded up. Once on a time fountains ran proud and free everywhere; now all are silenced.

What has brought about such a disastrous change? The answer lies in the shift of ownership that bankrupted the rich merchants, for Yucatán is the native habitat of a special type of cactus from which rope is made. The control of this important industry has become the property of the Mexican government and the income derived from the plantations goes to Mexico. With the decline of private wealth, the clerical party has fallen on evil days, and the churches, like the manor houses, are closed. One priest is allowed for every fifty miles and this rule is strictly enforced.

Our first visit was to Sr. Rube M. Romero, editor and owner of the only liberal newspaper in Yucatán. For his daring he has been stoned and more than once has had his equipment set on fire. He was most receptive to the Bahá'í ideals and listened to the Message with deep attention. He speaks no English and asked for the books in Spanish which he said he would gladly review in his paper. He accepted and published an article on the Bahá'í Religion, placing it on the front page.

Next we called at the Chamber of Commerce where Sr. N. Sarlet, the chairman, granted us an interview. He received us with courtesy but was noncommittal; his preoccupied manner was to become familiar to us while talking with prominent men of the city. It was an attitude of listening with apparent fear of hearing what might be said, a state of fear where no one dared make a decision, a great unwillingness to speak lest words be used against you.

Chichen Itza was our ultimate destination, a four hour ride from Mérida. The roads were incredibly bad; momentarily it seemed as though the wheels would fly off and the whole motor shake to pieces. The chauffeur, pained by our apprehension, assured us that this was considered a fine road and expressed surprise that we did not enjoy it. Finally, we drew up before the only inn at Chichen Itza which consisted of a main building surrounded by small adobe houses, each round and thatched. These are the rooms for guests. Vistas of the Mayan city could be seen through the trees. The work of restoration has been going on for almost a hundred years, and immediately after the war the Carnegie Institute sent a commission to complete the work. Though there are innumerable mounds yet untouched, a group of buildings that must have formed the central pivot of the city stands complete and perfect. The architecture is surprising, combining many forms which they could not have possibly seen — the field for games might have been built today, while ceremonial altars resemble ancient pyramids, the top gained by hundreds of steps built into each of its four sides, the plumed serpents having been carved to extend the entire length and form a balustrade as well as a symbolic ornament.

The "Temple of the Warriors," so named by the Carnegie commission, has six columns of figures, elaborately dressed in robes of state. It suggests a Greek Temple, while the tower for astronomical observations is round and might have been a mosque. As the Spanish Fathers burned all the Mayan records, little is known of the belief or even the customs of the people. No Rosetta stone has yet been found to decipher the hieroglyphics written on the stones. Perhaps it is this fact that acts upon the imagination and gives a special zest to the fragments one may gleam of this fascinating people.

There is a moment of supreme glory in every clime — the coming of day — but none can surpass the sunrise of Yucatán. Its most dramatic feature is caused by the heavy dew that rains down each night obscuring forest and glen and covering the ground until it looks as though a white sheet had been laid over it. The first shafts of light penetrate the thatch with long fingers, turning it into bright gold; showers of diamonds shake down from the trees, while scarfs of mist shot through with irridescent colors from the sun's rays float in the air. Then the dew lifts from the grass and like a magic carpet disappears. Jungle birds, wild with the joy of the coming day, try to reach the sun with their high notes and as the curtains of mist part, one building after another rises to greet the dawn as they did thousands of years ago.

Even today the proud descendants of the Mayans will not speak Spanish unless forced to, but they are glad to pick up English words and are friendly with strangers. The rainy season had just ended when we arrived and an army of workmen were repairing the adobe walls that melt away each year. Mayans will not work under an overseer. A man we would speak of as foreman, is referred to as the oldest friend of the Chichen Itza Inn, and it was this important person who extended to us hospitality and invited us to a supper given to celebrate Twelfth Night. We gladly accepted. His home, like that of his ancestors before him, was in the jungle. Each house is hidden by miles of vegetation. It is only when the moon is overhead that it is safe to enter the jungle at night. The roads are rough and winding and often their outline is lost. The depth of the forest affords them seclusion.

Twelfth Night fell at the full of the moon. Though dew was falling from myriads of leaves, we could see bits of sky above. A member of the family was sent to conduct us and from him we learned why there were no locks on the doors at Chichen Itza. He replied in answer to our question that his people had never desired what belongs to another — we can use only that which comes willingly to us. No Mayan settlement has ever permitted a lock and key. I asked if his people were Catholic. "To a certain extent only, but we remember the beliefs and sayings of our ancestors and hand them down from one generation to another." Presently the flares, from the house toward which we were moving, came into view. A Mayan house consists of two rooms separated by a

walled patio. One room holds all the family belongings while
the other is used for ceremonials. The patio is the kitchen and
living quarters. Both poor and rich sleep in hammocks. They
are swung at night and taken down in the day. The hammocks
of the poor are made of hemp but the well-to-do employ raw
silk with long knotted fringe that can be wrapped around one
for warmth. One hammock lasts a lifetime and is easily washed
and mended. The original price is high — for silk, sometimes a
thousand dollars. This reduces the cumbersome paraphernalia
of night to its simplest equation.

We were made welcome. Sweet smelling boughs had been
fastened over the door and on the walls of the patio. The hard
mud floor was not only swept but sprinkled with wild flowers
and a supper of tortillas was being prepared by many hands.
We were ushered into the ceremonial chamber and given seats.
Before us was an altar — very crude, made of unplaned boards.
The top board had long streamers of tissue paper representing
the visit of the Three Wise Men from the East to the infant
Savior. The middle shelf was Mayan with china dogs guardians of the law — very Chinese in effect. While the third tier
was Catholic in memory of the Spanish Fathers who toiled to
draw them to Christianity. On a lace background was a highly
colored picture of the Madonna of Guadelupe surrounded by
home-made candles. Opposite these mixed symbols we sat
down, one Englishman, one Mayan, two Spaniards and myself.
We gazed at the altar for a long time and nothing was said.

The Spaniard sitting next to me finally broke the silence
saying "What can one believe — how much in the past has been
true — how much false?" The Mayan asked, "Is it not the
ancestral belief that really holds the kernel of our religious
thought?" Beyond us in the patio noisy preparations were
going forward so we drew closer together that we might talk
unhampered. "We cannot jump into the middle of so ordered
a subject," I said, "we must go back and see what makes the
rhythm of evolution." "Well," replied the Spaniard, "we accept
only Christ either in the past or future." I answered, "Every

civilization has been founded on the coming of a great being. To the Hindu, that being is Bhudda; to the Zoroastrian, it is Zarathustra; to the Moslem it is Mohammed; to the Christian, Christ. But we believe that each was sent by Almighty God at a certain time with a message, without which mankind could progress no further. These Prophets represent the spiritual seasons; the appearance of one is the springtime. When his teachings penetrate the hearts of men it is the summer of that cycle, then the harvest appears and the precepts are fulfilled. Following the succession of the material seasons, eventually winter comes, when the religion is handed down and belief is accepted without question or ecstasy. Mental concepts obscure the love of God. Minds of limitation construct dogmas; forms and ceremonies creep in and become over-meaningly important. Belief is no longer fluid, it is like the ice of winter. The cold winds of dispute blow over the land and the seeker knows not where to turn for guidance.

"In such a dark hour comes the Illumined One; born under the laws of nature; arising from a despised people of the remote East. He walks among men and where he steps the earth blossoms. The Word is made flesh and dwells amongst us. The new light creating a higher vibration crumbles barriers and traditions — governments fall — idols are overthrown. But seeing eyes glimpse the vision of a new day. The moment arrived for such a being and Bahá'u'lláh has come to recreate all things and make them new." Again there was silence. In the silence I began repeating the Greatest Name of God as given by Bahá'u'lláh.

At the utterance of the Title of God the walls of the dwelling about us dissolved. The heart of the jungle lay bare. With some inner perception I beheld an ancient people. They were coming from all directions and were of all ages. They were listening to the Great Name of God. Even as the multitudes gathered to hear the Sermon on the Mount and the wild Arabs of the desert followed Mohammed, so the Mayan people seemed to respond to the call of this New Day. Past and present were swept together in an instant of reality shot from heaven to earth.

What passed in the minds of the men around me, I did not know, but they too seemed changed. We looked at each other with understanding, and were drawn together by a spirit that had pushed back the curtain of time and revealed eternity.

When we were summoned to the feast and the spell was broken, we entered the patio in a thoughtful mood. For those assembled it was Twelfth Night, the ancient celebration, but for us it was a new rejoicing. Something had changed that words were powerless to explain, but each heart would carry away a message that would throw light where before had been darkness.

Chapter 26

MEXICO

We came to Veracruz from Yucatán and proceeded to Mexico City but it is not of that journey I write, since illness and disaster blotted it out. In 1949 I again went to Mexico City. This time I was a delegate from the Inter-America Committee to the Latin America Congress.

On the below zero and snowy morning of January first Ophelia Crum (driving the car), Kay Zinky, and I left Colorado Springs. We had heard that drinking water was doubtful so we had filled several demijohns with sparkling water from Manitou Springs — wrapped ourselves in wool and fur and set off. We had not gone far when we heard a series of explosions somewhere in our rear. Upon investigation we discovered the floor of the trunk covered with chunks of ice and bits of glass. Thus ended precaution number one, and we decided to take no provision for the morrow. We got in and wrapped up again, when "snap-snap" went the chains on all four wheels. Shorn of all protection, we drove in grim silence all that day over a glaze of ice! The Mexican mountains have on the crest a hundred miles of twisted turns and by the time one descends, a flat stretch of road looks like paradise.

Nothing takes so much time and absorbs so much energy as a Congress, yet nothing is more difficult to describe. "What did you do at the Congress?" people ask; and you reply, "We talked about plans for teaching; we reviewed the history of the Faith;" and then you stop because you are not giving any true picture or brushing in the special colors, that the Congress

99

had. We saw old friends and new and our beloved Marcia
Steward was present; and where Marcia is there is drama.

At this time the U. N. were holding meetings in the City
and this fact played into our hands in a remarkable manner.
We had many colored members of our Congress and I asked
the manager of the hotel for the use of the music room to
entertain our delegates. He seemed indifferent to this request
at first, then suddenly was all attention, offering us the yellow
ballroom free of charge. We gave a party in the grand manner.
What had happened was that he thought us delegates from the
U. N. — which hurt no one and benefitted us greatly.

Each delegate asked for an interview with me alone and
so I gave my evenings for this purpose. The heart-searching
questions were centered in the teachings — not a single personal problem was broached — and my memory of our private
talks is filled by the vigor of the spirit of the Latin people.

Chapter 27

CENTRAL AMERICA AND PIONEERING EFFORTS

Journeying through Central America was less rewarding than travelling in South America, where we meandered along at our own leisure. Here tours had to be taken in fruit boats and that meant time in port was limited. The perishable cargoes were loaded and at once the ships hurried on. Thus our glimpses of Central American cities were fleeting. When we reached the harbor of Costa Rica with its beauteous panorama of islands, time was too short for the train ride to San Jose. Instead we poked about the dusty port, peering into doorways and shops and wondering how people existed without shade, a tint of green or a book to read. In the same abbreviated manner we reached three Islands — Trinidad, Jamaica and Cuba. Marion Little and I had been invited by the American Ambassador and his wife to spend a week with them in Havana. "What an opportunity to teach!" we said to each other. Alas, the people who came to dine or who gave garden parties and teas were not in the slightest bit interested. At the first mention of religion they commenced to yawn prodigiously and were only revived by hearing that I knew Mary Pickford and Douglas Fairbanks. We were puzzled by these rebuffs and loudly lamented our failures. We had not learned that those who seek the spirit have been unchained from the pleasures of the world.

When the journeys ended we settled down to the business of how best to send out pioneers to Latin America. I went to Washington. Through the kindness of Mason Remey I obtained an interview with the Secretary of State, Cordell Hull. I explained our plans and why we were sending what he called "missionaries" to the Southern Countries. Both unity of race and religion appealed to him and he promised to endorse our efforts. In turn he advised the study of the health laws that differed in each country and for this advice the Committee was grateful in the days to come. I determined to talk with Prof. Lewis Hanke who had charge of the Cultural Division of the Congressional Library. We had corresponded when he was head of Latin America literature at Harvard College and now was my chance for a personal conference. He gave me the names of five volumes that he considered indispensable to the understanding of the people of Latin America. They were *The Gulf of Misunderstanding, The Other Spanish Christ,* two handbooks by Latin American authors, and Prescott's *South America.*

The pioneers were moving southward and the burning question now arose — how should our books find their way to them? There was the problem of postal regulations — and there was the costly postage. This apparently unsolvable problem melted miraculously before the generous offer of Mr. O'Hanion. He was an old friend of Frances Stewart and when he heard of our dilemma he offered to be our agent. Through a believer, Mr. Filipac, a steward on a steamship going back and forth to Brazil, a few books at a time were delivered in Rio de Janeiro. He carried them to II Ave Rio Branco in Rio, and through business connections Mr. O'Hanion sent them all over South America, even as far as Chili. Thus we invaded Latin America! Heartbreaking disappointments were strewn along the path and delays both long and short were dotted like punctuations throughout our efforts. But there were higher powers at work in our behalf that triumphed over the setbacks. These setbacks were realized by the Guardian as shown by the exchange of early cables. I reprint one of our first cables to Shoghi Effendi, and his reply:

> "Ask prayers Inter-America work
> Spanish translations delayed
> Panama and Nicaragua posts filled."

To which the Guardian replied:

> "Delighted. Praying that
> remaining obstacles will
> be removed. Loving gratitude.
> (Signed)   Shoghi"

I would like to mention the names of all those who con-tributed to upbuilding of the Faith throughout Latin America but in this limited space only the names of the earliest pioneers can be recorded. Those who followed furthered the same praiseworthy purpose and many are living there today.

First went Katherine Frankland and her husband, who in 1912 journeyed to Mexico City at the request of 'Abdu'l-Bahá. In 1919 Martha Root made her famous trip and she was followed that same year by Leonora Holsapple Armstrong who settled in Bahia, Brazil. The Louis Gregorys spent several months in Haiti in 1934. Mrs. Joel Stebbins and Isabel Dodge taught in Peru in 1936. The Roy Worleys, Eve Nicklin, Bea-trice Irwin and Frances Stewart pioneered in 1937. In 1938 Mr. and Mrs. Ward Calhoon went to Havana. In 1939 we received the appeal of the Guardian through *The Advent of Divine Justice* and in response those who went that year were: Louise Caswell, Cora Oliver, Mathew Kaszab, Gayle Woolson, Margaret Lentz, the John Shaws, Antonio Roca, John Eichen-auer, Jr., Clarence Iverson, Wilford Barton, Roheieh Jones, Katherine Disdier, and John Stearns.

Remembering our weak beginnings not yet twenty years past, it is startling to realize that we have today two National Spiritual Assemblies in Latin America, elected by their own delegates. Dorothy Baker, our last chairman, carried forward the work like a tidal wave. When the moment came for this apex of achievement I could not attend and sent a cable ad-dressed to my children to which they replied, "Your children growing up fast — our love to you." Our spiritual heirs show both sincerity and maturity as was witnessed by Ophelia Crum and I when we travelled to Havana and Jamaica last winter (1951). We found groups as well as Assemblies, earnestly studying the Bahá'í writings and full of spiritual "growing pains."

We cannot close an outline of the work done in the Continent below us without thinking of May Maxwell who gave her life and her talents to the Faith and finally journeyed to Argentina to teach, and died in that faraway land.

Part Four
The Invisible World

Chapter 28

AN INSPIRATION

"It is an axiomatic fact that while you meditate you are speaking with your own spirit. In that state of mind you put certain questions to your spirit and your spirit answers: the light breaks forth and reality is revealed."

Tablet on Meditation
'Abdu'l-Bahá

I awoke one morning at dawn. It was in the Summer of 1939. A carnival of light flooded the valley at the foot of Pike's Peak. In the presence of the oncoming day one has no memories. The sun is rising and you stand witness to a new creation. Meditation is the natural mode of thought in this half conscious, half unconscious state. As I watched the hills lose their shadows and sharpen against the sky line a message flashed across space into my heart. "These acres have a high purpose — above the need of family or friend, here shall come the nations in a new comradeship. They shall meet here and become a common denominator for the future of mankind."

Once the inspiration was mine it gave me no rest until I had opened the house as a Bahá'í International School. I invited the older believers to help formulate a policy that would be suitable for foreign students. At the opening Shoghi Effendi cabled, "Delighted — praying for success, loving appreciation." In a letter to Max and Inez Greeven, assisting me in the formation of the school, the Guardian wrote: "The courses of the school should be planned in such a way as to exert the greatest possible influence on the progress of the teaching work now going forward so well in the countries of the South."

In 1947, with the consent of my husband and my daughter, Wanden Kane, the estate was deeded to the National Spiritual Assembly of the Bahá'ís of the United States. I asked that the supervision be offered to Margaret Randall Ford, daughter of my cousin Harry Randall, who was not only related to me but who had been a close friend of my husband's. The Guardian confirmed the appointment. With true pioneer spirit Harry Ford, Margaret's husband, set to work on the grounds, tilting with the inanimate objects of every size and shape; moving rocks from the ground, building walls and fences and bridges. They toiled incessantly for the upbuilding of the school, and now in 1951 its doors are open and I pray may never close.

Chapter 29

A DREAM

"If we ponder each created thing, we shall witness a myriad
perfect wisdoms and learn a myriad new and wondrous truths.
One of the created phenomena is the dream. Behold how
many secrets are deposited therein. Observe how thou art
asleep in a dwelling, its doors barred; on a sudden thou findest
thyself in a far-off city which thou enterest without moving thy
feet or wearying thy body; without using thine eyes, thou
seest; without taxing thine ears, thou hearest; without a tongue
thou speakest. Perchance when ten years are gone, thou wilt
witness in the outer world the very things thou has dreamed
tonight."   — Bahá'u'lláh

How are we to distinguish between the dream of which
Bahá'u'lláh speaks and the fleeting images of the night? There
is one infallible rule — a dream fades. No matter how vivid
the images and impressions are, a few hours of wakefulness
blurs their clarity and every passing moment sends them
further and further into obscurity. A vision is etched on the
conscious mind and framed on the walls of memory. The
details neither diminish nor increase — the imprint is timeless.
The dream I relate was of such a fabric. Its reality took years
to unfold, as the Prophet tells us "Perchance when ten years
are gone." From this we gather that time is a non-essential
factor in true vision.

It happened before the journey to South America during
a short visit to Honolulu. I remember thinking with great
satisfaction that there was a strong Assembly here and many
workers in the Bahá'í field and I was not needed. The more

vigorously I brushed my hair the more assured I felt of my right to leisure. In this un-Bahá'í state of mind I fell asleep. Suddenly the door between the lanai and my bedroom opened and 'Abdu'l-Bahá looking stern and none too well pleased with me, moved swiftly across the floor. "I have many friends here who do not know me. Come." As Bahá'u'lláh describes in the quotation, we moved, yet without motion, and found ourselves in an enclosure at one end of which was a hospital and we were standing under a stone arch facing it. A young nurse dressed in a uniform descended the steps of the building. She seemed in distress and catching sight of the Master she ran towards him crying: "Oh, 'Abdu'l-Bahá! Must I go — is it my duty — can't someone else be sent instead of me? It's so bleak — so dreary there." 'Abdu'l-Bahá took a step towards her and cast a glance of loving sympathy that would have melted the heart of a stone, but he uttered no word. The picture seemed to retreat and then to fade away. Again without motion or seeming volition we came to a hillside. It was covered with trees and flowers and under an oak tree we were standing, evidently waiting on some happening. Before us was an old-fashioned house with a large white front door and three stone steps that led down into the garden in which we were standing. Presently the door was pushed open and a women dressed in soft white material that fluttered about her as she moved stepped down one stone, paused as though fearing to be observed, looked in one direction and then in another until she perceived the Master. She uttered a cry, folding her hands on her breast and in a voice of suppressed emotion, addressed him: "Oh, I did not know you were here, 'Abdu'l-Bahá! Tell me, is what I am about to do right? Have I your sanction? I am so worried; I do not know if I should proceed with my plan or not." So saying, she pointed to a clump of young trees growing on the right side of the house. The Master stood perfectly still, paused and then in a clear voice said "Permission is granted, and it will not fail of its purpose." Again the hillside, the garden; the woman retreated from our vision and

presently we were travelling in an entirely different part of
the Island. I seemed to be aware that the cottage before me
was that of an artist. One who did not know of the Faith but
one whom the Master loved. The man was sitting at an easel
and the Master came and stood beside him and put his arm
around his shoulder. In a hammock on the lanai was a boy
about sixteen. He was reading a book and swinging himself
back and forth — he was notably handsome. The Master began
talking to the artist; his tone was serious though kindly. "Do
not be frightened at what your son will be called upon to per-
form in the war. It is dangerous but he will have protection.
You must remain calm and show no fear. Do not try to dis-
suade him from his duty. Go your way and he must go his."

Three years later, in World War II, the boy became a
dive bomber, the most perilous occupation in the Navy. He
passed through this ordeal unscathed.

The next two years was spent in travel and then we came
again to the lovely Island of Oahu. The friends were holding
their public meetings in the Y.W.C.A. and they asked me to
speak. In the front row sat the woman of the three stone steps
(as I had named her in my mind). She was dressed in deep
mourning and looked paler than on the night of my vision.
She came forward after the talk and introduced herself.

"I have lost my husband," she explained, "and am searching for some answer to the after life. I came to your meeting
thinking that the Bahá'í Faith might throw new light on this
subject." I assured her that it did contain many new revela-
tions on eternal life that are both satisfying and consoling.

Nearly every day until my departure for China she came
to talk over the many facets of the teaching and when I left
she was deep in study of the Faith. I was not surprised, therefore, to receive a letter the following Autumn asking the date
of our arrival and announcing her entrance into the Faith
awaiting my arrival. As we drew near the wharf with the
lovely song of greeting "Aloha" floating out on the water, I
saw Florence — a lei of scented flowers in her hands — a radiant

expression on her face. Marion Little was standing beside me
and I longed to tell her of the dream since we shared every
experience, yet something withheld me. I felt the moment
was propitious for me to ask Florence the meaning of the
ambiguous scene I had witnessed. With this intent I went
alone to her house determined to re-enact the dream. I made
her open the front door and walk down one step and there
pause. I stood under the oak tree just as I had that night.
"Florence, two years ago I came here in a dream — I was with
'Abdu'l-Bahá. You opened the front door and stood on the
step — where you are standing now. Perceiving the Master
you asked his permission for something you contemplated
doing — it concerned those small trees growing there on the
right of the house." At these words Florence sank down on the
step and covered her face. "No, no," she cried, "no one knows
that — no one could know it!" I waited while she recovered
her composure, she lifted her head and sighed. "What you
saw that night is true. But a secret not even my children know.
When I decided to enter the Faith I had my husband moved
from the graveyard on the hill and placed him under the
little trees he had planted and tended with so much care."

The drama of the trees had taken place before Florence's
study of the Bahá'í teachings and at a time when her husband
was in perfect health. Perhaps in the flux of life there is no
past or future as we know them. Destiny may complete itself
in the same manner that the branches of an oak are present
in the acorn; as the harvest is wrapped in the seed. Our
sequence of time — the succession of days and nights so im-
perative in our daily life may not exist in the invisible world.
In that world life may be a continuous flow ever merging in
a timeless sea. Who knows?

Three more years passed before I met the nurse I had seen
on that memorable night. She was a Bahá'í but had been
working on another Island so I had never seen her. During
the evening she whispered to me that she had a problem and
wanted to ask my advice. When we had moved apart from

the others she told me she had been asked to take a position as nurse at the Leper Settlement of Molokai.

"I hate the idea," she said, "but as a Bahá'í have I the right to refuse? Someone must go in my place if I stay at home." Remembering 'Abdu'l-Bahá's silence, I knew I must not interfere in her final decision. "Let us say the Ahmad Tablet for nine days — meet, and talk it over again." When we came together, every trace of indecision had been wiped from her mind. "I have resolved to go," she cried, "and since I talked with you I have been there and had such a different impression that I am sure I will not be unhappy." "Your decision is final?" I asked. "Yes, yes" — she looked as though she contemplated leaving that instant. "Wait one moment before you go," I said, laughing at her impatience. "I want to tell you that you asked 'Abdu'l-Bahá the same question four years ago." "What did he reply?" I wondered how best to explain it. "He did not reply but left the decision to you." She went to Molokai. While in the hospital she met the Commissioner of the Institutions of the Hawaiian Islands. They fell in love, married, and, like the fairy stories of our childhood, lived happily ever after.

I learned from this experience the brittle quality of personal opinion. The Master with His penetration of ethereal substance knew that the woman must make the choice that involved her destiny. What appeared as a sacrifice contained her future life that she must accept or reject. But our insight is limited — and we cannot know with any degree of positive knowledge. We surmise, we imagine, as though blindfolded we aim at a target. Why do we trust our judgment so implicitly? Life is so rich in good counsels but oh, how poor in knowledge of the human heart.

Chapter 30

A MIRACLE

While 'Abdu'l-Bahá was visiting Lady Bloomfield in London a caller approached him saying:

"There must be miracles in the Bahá'í Faith. Many miracles, are there not?" "Yes, of course," replied the Master, "many miracles but miracles have frequently obscured the teachings which the Divine Messengers have brought. The Message is the real miracle. Phenomenal miracles are unimportant, they prove nothing to anyone but the witness thereof, even they will often explain them away! Therefore miracles have no value in the teaching of religion."

— *The Chosen Highway*

During our many treks to Honolulu it was my privilege to talk often with Elizabeth Mouther. Though she was old when I knew her she was still highly vitalized. She was living out her last days in the house of Katherine Baldwin at 36 Bates Street. Little by little I gathered the threads of her life. She had come from Illinois and as a young girl had become an enthusiastic Bahá'í. A call had come from the Hawaiian Islands for teachers to instruct the children of the missionaries. She had offered to go and, in a sailing vessel, had embarked on what was then a long voyage. Elizabeth had a guileless quality that seems to be one of the attributes of those who recognize a new Messenger. It is a peculiar quality that makes one understand what Jesus meant in saying we must become as little children. Alone in a far-off world Elizabeth began writing 'Abdu-'l-Bahá, pouring out her heart, telling him of her longing for marriage, children and a domestic life. She explained her isolated existence and how there was no oppor-

115

tunity for social contacts. 'Abdu'l-Bahá in reply wrote her of
the wonders of this day and of his own station; that station
that would not be understood until far in the future when
his words had rolled to the corners of the earth. After wrestling
with her problems Elizabeth wrote that she would sacrifice
her personal life for the good of the children and stay indefi-
nitely on the Islands. In reply 'Abdu'l-Bahá wrote an astonishing letter; he said in substance, that for her sacrifice she
would be permitted a glimpse of life beyond the mortal veil
and she would be a witness to the reality of eternal life and
the continuance of the soul. This was to be in nine years from
that time.

Elizabeth did not grasp the meaning of his words. How,
she thought, could I see another plane while I am still on
earth? Nevertheless, the mysterious document, containing
promises she did not understand — words that were beyond
her comprehension — was placed in a box of sandalwood
under lock and key. Sometimes in the evening when her work
was done, she would unlock the case, take out the letter and
read over the strange and wonderful words written by the
Master.

When she reached this point she paused and told me that
I was not at liberty to relate this secret chapter during her
lifetime. I promised. Then she resumed.

At the time of which she spoke she was nursery governess
to a boy of three years — a lovely child and especially precious
as a babe in arms had died just before his birth. The boy,
Richard, had a great affection for Uttie, as he called her. The
years spent on the Island of Maui with Richard were the hap-
piest of her life and intense was her grief and loneliness when
at the age of eleven he was sent to boarding school on the
mainland. When vacation time came there was rejoicing,
goodies were cooked, games played and the house rang with
gaiety and laughter.

Thus the years slipped by when out of a cloudless sky
tragedy fell. In a cable the fateful words reached them. While

on the playing field Richard had been struck with a baseball and killed. A cruiser was commissioned to bring the body of the beloved child to Honolulu and proceed to Maui for burial.

Trembling, Elizabeth took out the Tablet and spread it on her lap. Blinded by tears she could scarcely read the well-known words. Here was the date — just nine years had elapsed. When she looked up a translucent light had spread around her blotting out the familiar objects and to her surprise she saw Richard. He was dressed in blue denim shorts and a white shirt open at the neck. She was aware of an ugly gash on his forehead. "Oh Uttie," he cried, "I have come home. I have tried to tell mother that I am not badly hurt but she will not listen to me but goes on sobbing and moaning. I am all right, Uttie, but I won't go to Maui — promise me you won't go either. I'll stay here with you and bring my brother to play — he is a big boy now and you will like to see him."

Uttie sat in her rocking chair transfixed — how long she did not know. Her next conscious moment was seeing Richard's mother standing in the doorway telling her to prepare to leave for Maui early in the morning. "Please forgive me," Elizabeth said, "I cannot go." "But you must go, Uttie." In a low weak voice, Uttie replied "I cannot go to Maui." Baffled, bewildered, and deeply hurt, the mother withdrew.

Elizabeth sat in her room alone. The house was silent, for every member of the household had departed for Maui. In the early afternoon the strange yellow light that had previously enveloped the room now extended across the garden paths. Even before Uttie looked up she was aware that the children were beside her. The mark on Richard's brow had faded. He was so familiar and real that she could scarcely refrain from taking him in her arms. "Oh Uttie, I am so glad you did not go to Maui — you would never have seen Charles and isn't it fun being here together, just we three." A shadow crossed out the smiles as he took a step nearer, "Uttie why could not mother talk to me — was it because she was crying?" Uttie replied gently, "It is not possible at this time Richard, perhaps

later." Richard interrupted, "I tried to tell her I was not hurt —
that is, it was only for a moment — there was nothing to carry
on so about." The boys ran into the garden and Elizabeth
heard their happy voices calling one to another.

This was the fulfillment of 'Abdu'l-Bahá's promise. Richard
the child was hers on a plane not of this physical world. To
her he had returned to confide his secrets and his meeting with
his brother. She alone shared his happiness. Never had Elizabeth doubted the eternal quality of life but this vivid proof
was a living knowledge that quickened the pulse and sang
through the blood, lifted her being into the fountain of eternal
life.

> "When a certain child passed away, 'Abdu'l-Bahá said to the
> mother: 'There is a Garden of God. Human beings are trees
> growing therein. The Gardener is our Father. When He sees
> a little tree in a place too small for its development, He pre-
> pares a suitable and a more beautiful place, where it may
> grow and bear fruit. Then He transplants that little tree.'"
>
> — The Chosen Highway

Part Five
Across the Seven Seas

Chapter 31

ISLANDS OF THE SOUTHERN HEMISPHERE

Tahiti

The hour had arrived, long ago promised by 'Abdu'l-Bahá, that I should cross the Seven Seas. The *Franconia* was already in sight, her graceful outline a joy to look upon.

We left Honolulu and plunged down across the equator into the Southern Hemisphere; stars hidden in Northern skies were on display; playful dolphins tumbled in the waves as they followed in our wake; the sea no longer indigo, grew paler each day and its rollers passed by slowly and evenly, as though spaced by a tape. The Tiare flower sends out waves of perfume to greet you long before you sight land. This small flower, a near relative of the orange blossom, covers the Island with its piquant fragrance and pushes its way among the brilliant bougainvilles vines. Louise and John Bosch who had spent some time on the Island had given me an address of a shopkeeper and his wife whom they had interested in the Faith. When I arrived at the door, a padlock hung there ominously and iron shutters covered the windows. This was my first disappointment.

Erstwhile I joined a group of native girls on their way to bathe — not by the sea as I had expected, but on a high plateau crowned by a waterfall that sent a crystal stream of water over the ledges into a smooth round basin below. The girls shook out their long braids and drenched them beneath the falling water. They picked leaves not unlike our furry mullein with which they dried the long strands of brown hair.

121

For brilliantine they squeezed oil from the Tiare flower and rubbed it briskly over their tresses until they shone in the sun. Instead of jewelry, they wove fresh flowers into chains and bracelets, reserving the red tulips for earrings; they wore only a sarong — that practical garment with its deep pockets and voluminous folds. Together we descended the hill towards the harbor. .

At five we sailed away from the land of romance and story, the girls waving and throwing kisses from the shore. The sea reflected the pastel shades of the setting sun, and one could believe in the sorceries and superstitions of this enchanted Isle. The sea now empty and vague made you wonder if you had actually visited this scented oasis or only dreamed it!

Rarotonga, Cook Islands

Three hundred Europeans lived on this Island because of its salubrious climate. This was, of course, before World War II. A native dwelling consists of a wooden platform with a post at each corner. To each post tapa cloth is tied that can be dropped down to insure privacy or raised to extend the view. Tapa, one of the most beautiful as well as serviceable materials in the world, is made from Mulberry bark. It is impervious to rain and insects, and is stencilled in a great variety of designs. I brought home pieces of tapa with which I papered the library of the International School. On the platform of one native house I saw an ancient sewing machine, salvaged, probably, from a mission bungalow. It was displayed, as one might a relic from antiquity. The owner had no inkling of its purpose, believing it to be purely ornamental.

Tin Can Island

Mail for "Niuafoou" is sealed in a biscuit tin and thrown overboard to a swimmer who waits in the water and who has brought out-going mail through the sea to the ship. This process is repeated twice a year and is responsible for the nickname of the Island. Stamps from "Niuafoou" are a collectors' item.

Suva, Fiji Islands

Suva, situated at the crossroads of the Pacific, is thought to have a great future. Moreover the Fijis, since embracing Christianity, have become teachable and docile. In the last century King Thakpombau, ruler of the Tribe, sent to Queen Victoria a war club in token of their submission to the English Crown, and King George V, having discovered this famous club in the palace of Windsor in 1931, returned it to Suva for use in Government meetings. Some years ago The Rockefeller Foundation sent a contingent of doctors and nurses to stamp out hookworm in the Fiji Islands. Dr. S. M. Lambert who headed the expedition has written a delightful book entitled *Twenty Years in Paradise*, describing life in the Islands. With an English Doctor, Aubrey Montague, they opened a medical school for the natives — this was in 1928. They discovered an aptitude in the Fijis for both medicine and surgery. They trained the men as doctors, the women as nurses, and Dr. Lambert declares that many Europeans have been saved by native doctors, especially in remote Islands. The Fijis were also found to have an almost perfect ear for harmony. For Bahá'í pioneers this is an important lesson in fostering the talents in groups of people while visiting strange lands.

Apia, Samoan Islands

The harbor of Apia is perilous in stormy weather. In 1889 seven warships were lost here in a single hurricane. Today, however, it was calm as a millpond and it was difficult to picture its treachery. We were met by a Mr. Walker, who had come to greet us because of mutual friends in Australia. He was brought to Apia as headmaster of the Fiji Boys School and his enthusiasm for the work and for the qualities of the boys knew no bounds. Long before we reached the hilltop where the school was situated he had told us the story of Robert Louis Stevenson's devotion to the Island people.

Stevenson came to Apia after the great storm of 1889 and took the only house suitable for a white man's family (the house now used as the Regency). As he looked over the property with the agent he noticed a number of signs on which were written the word "Kapoc." "What does that mean?" queried Stevenson. "That says, 'Keep Out' — it prevents the natives from trespassing — they dare not encroach when they see that sign."

The agent departed. Stevenson found two boards and printed in the Fiji tongue, "Come in, Robert Louis Stevenson is always at home."

The natives padded up, read the sign, and retreated; but one bolder than the others pushed open the gate, came to the veranda steps and sat down. This was the beginning of a deep and lifelong friendship between the Fiji chiefs and Stevenson. He not only admired their qualities but fought for their rights. The Vailima Letters were written for this purpose. Finding that they were frequently imprisoned without reason Stevenson journeyed to London to plead their cause before Parliament. It was during this visit to London that the natives searched the Islands for sods of grass and laid them down from the main road of the Island to Stevenson's gate, upon which the welcome sign was placed. This road is still kept fresh and is known as "The road of the Loving Heart."

The friendship of a single white man during this dark chapter of Fiji history resulted in moulding anew the lives of the people. One shower of understanding love opened a new world to the savages and the change that occured was little short of miraculous.

"You will hear the grandsons of these chieftains sing. We have translated the words of popular songs into Fiji — you will be astonished when you hear them," quoth our guide.

In the school grounds the boys were playing cricket, their dark skins set off by white sarongs and each one had a jonquil behind his ear. Their ages ranged from twelve to sixteen and they had the mops of bushy hair that marks the Fiji tribes. Their eyes were coal black with finely marked brows and they were tall and well built. They were evidently expecting us and, at once, left their game and took their places according to the part they were to sing. They began their repertoire with an ancient Samoan boat song, followed by a chant for fair weather, afterwards came a group of American Songs, among them "There's a Long, Long Trail," "Pack Up Your Troubles" and "My Old Kentucky Home." Mr. Walker singled out one of the older boys who was studying English to tell us of their last and most important song.

He began, "Our people had a friend. His name was Robert Louis Stevenson and he came to Apia when the Chiefs, our grandparents, were sorely tried. They came to know the white man that had come to live among them and with him they felt safe. He taught them many things they had not known and best of all was about comradeship. He wrote books and sometimes songs and he wrote the verse that is engraved on the boulder at the top of the hill in front of you. When he died only the Fiji Chiefs were strong enough to carry him aloft where he asked to be laid. That verse on the grave we were taught in our own language but thinking about the words we wondered what they were in English and so after a while we asked to learn it in the language in which our little father Stevenson wrote it." The boys rose, held up their hands towards the heights above and in a low key sang:

> "Under the wide and starry sky,
> Dig the grave and let me lie
> Glad did I live and gladly die,
> And I laid me down with a will.
> This be the verse you grave for me;
> Here he lies where he longed to be.
> Home is the sailor, home from the sea,
> And the hunter home from the hill."

Java

Java belonged to the Dutch before the last war when I saw it in 1936. It was a green world with a hundred and forty volcanic mountains rising from the deep valleys. This is the land of Batik, a material made by dipping cotton in melted wax and pressing a metal stamp on one side of the cloth thus imprinting the pattern on the other; this lovely stuff serves rich and poor and makes the clothes for both sexes.

The gamelan orchestra consisting of thirty instruments, mostly percussion, may be heard in every town and village. There is always one violin and one flute to carry the melody while the other instruments underwrite the theme with strange wild sounds.

The religion of the people is a form of Islam but differs greatly from the main beliefs, as ancient ideas and ceremonies of India are mingled with those of Mohammedan origin. In a hill at Borobudur was found a Temple of Buddhistic origin considered by archaeologists the most perfect example extant.

In Batavia I found without difficulty "The Olivier Brothers" bookstore to which I had been recommended. With gracious good will they accepted the books that I had brought in Dutch with me and not only promised to place them in circulation but asked that I send future translations when they appeared in print. This noble encouragement sent me back to the steamer in a state of ecstasy. Then World War II fell upon the people and with it our communication with our new found friends ceased.

Bali

Every Kingdom has its own perfection. The Mineral Kingdom has its jewels, the Vegetable Kingdom its roses, the Animal Kingdom its nightingales, and the Human Kingdom the Messengers from on high. I think the land too has its grades of both beauty and goodness. When I think of Bali it suggests a Byzantine mosaic, a Pagan Utopia which, indeed, it was. There had never been a crime on the Island, nor a prison nor a guardian of the law. Youth goes to the rice fields garlanded in lilies and returns to play music that has enthralled musicians all over the world. Here, through Millie Collins, I found an artist and his wife who were familiar with the Bahá'í Faith. They received me warmly and we talked of the response they were sure the people of Bali would make when the pamphlets I had brought were translated into High and Low Bali. It is sad that I have forgotten their name, but I have not forgotten their cordiality and the talks we had together, sitting in a garden that faced the sea, planning to bring a glimpse of heaven's glory to the Balinese.

Then came war. The military party in Japan were in control and they marched into Bali — what happened I had no means of knowing — only that my letters were returned to me. Did my friends have time to translate the Bahá'í Message into Low Bali? Were they taken prisoners or did they escape? I do not know and I have not been able to return.

Chapter 32

OPINIONS DIFFER

I *argued* with a minister and his wife brought to the *Franconia* by Agnes Alexander at Yokohama, Japan. Jesus was the only Divine Being ever to tread the earth, they claimed, while Agnes and I vigorously insisted that revelation was progressive, evolutionary and continuous.

I *argued* with the Zoroastrian Priests in Bombay, India; they stated that no one can become a Zoroastrian — one must be born in the Faith. I refuted this statement that physical birth controlled spiritual decision. Growth and progress bring about evolution in the human kingdom. The Priest at the head of the line shook his head sadly. No one answered. "I know the writings of your Prophet and I know you cannot substantiate your statement. The answer is — 'Tradition'!" And I hope they thought it over!

I *argued* with a Prince of Siam while in Bankok. We sat gazing at the emerald Buddha; it is beautiful as only a religious psyche can be. One actually feels the repose of meditation flowing out from him. It was an unforgettable experience. The Prince was an Oxford graduate. "Christianity," he said, had "failed to attract him since he did not feel in Jesus the divine model of Buddha." But each Messenger of God has a special mission; each adds the perfection of some quality; each gives the world the knowledge that will build a more advanced civilization. Buddha developed the meditative faculty; Jesus, love; and Bahá'u'lláh has proclaimed unity as the goal for this age.

129

I *argued* with a Coolie in Shanghai who scorned honesty — far from being the best policy, he believed it was stupid. The wise man feathered his nest — no matter by what means. The result, I assured him, of dishonesty would in time be chaos, confusion and ultimate destruction — truth being the jewel at the core of collective life that insures individual preservation. "Well, maybe I should not steal for myself, but if I steal for you isn't that brotherly love?" "Then we might both go to jail," I laughingly replied, "you as a thief, I as the recipient of stolen goods. When we were freed, no one would trust us, no one would employ us and we would become fugitives." "Maybe you're right, lady, I'll think it over," and he helped me down from the rickshaw, remarking that he would call on me aboard the boat, so that we could talk further. He came but I do not know what his final reaction was!

I *argued* with a prisoner on the Island of Mindanao in the prison of Zamboanga. He was paying the penalty of a life sentence for a moment of blind passion. He felt the verdict unjust and lived in a state of rebellion. I repeated the words of 'Abdu'l-Bahá in regard to his own imprisonment, "There is no prison save the prison of self." "It is beautiful on this Island and you are only shut up at night. You must learn to enjoy the degree of liberty that you have — in the sky and in the sea, the hand of the Creator is visible. Help your fellow prisoners and find a friend among them. Though you have a life sentence, God is able to strike off your chains. Promise me that you will read, every day, from the books I am leaving with you and have faith."

When the Japanese took the Island many prisoners escaped — perhaps this man among them. In my heart I believe he is free though I have no positive knowledge.

Everywhere I travelled I argued that the Greatest Event in history had occurred, again an Illumined One had walked the earth creating a higher vibration and crumbling barriers and traditions.

Chapter 33

WE REACH AUSTRALIA

The magnificent harbor of Sydney is fathoms deep, allowing vessels to anchor at the wharfs. A suspension bridge of lacy ironwork crosses one end of the bay. The port bristles with swaying masts and tugs in furious commotion. The wharfs are piled high with bales and boxes of every conceivable shape; whistles blow, chains rattle and cranes swing with their burdens and one feels the rhythm of exchange between east and west.

In my pocket I carried the address of the Bahá'í Center which was not far from the pier where we were berthed. I had no difficulty in finding it and slipped into a seat in the rear of the hall. On the platform was Hyde Dunn reading from *The Foundations of World Unity* by 'Abdu'l-Bahá.

As I sat there fragments of his life passed before me. How at one time Hyde had heard that 'Abdu'l-Bahá said "Would that I could go to Australia — even barefooted and in poverty — and speak of the Promised One who has come." In response to that appeal Mr. and Mrs. Dunn, though elderly and poor, embarked. In spite of drawbacks they thrived and in the first year Hyde heard an inner voice telling him to write to a certain firm in Melbourne and ask for a position. The answer was not long in coming; he was authorized to travel throughout the cities of Australia. A remarkable man, Mr. Whiterker by name, had joined the Faith in Sydney and whenever Mr. Dunn was away he taught the classes and promoted the work.

When the Cause was firmly established both in Melbourne and Adelaide this indomitable couple set out across the Great

131

Desert to Perth where they met Martha Root on her maiden voyage round the world. They had come in 1919 and now in 1936 a National Spiritual Assembly was in process of formation. Thus it was that Bahá'u'lláh spread a magic carpet for His disciples and placed in their hands the key of a continent.

A number of the friends walked back to the boat with me that night and I remember we spoke of the Guardian, his grasp of conditions in every part of the world, his ceaseless energy and loving understanding of our weaknesses as well as our efforts.

A youth meeting was arranged for the following evening. I was introduced by the Mayor's son and spoke on "The Goal of the New World Order." Young Australia showed a healthy mind and asked questions about proofs — authority for the Bahá'í words and principles. So vital was the discussion that it was midnight before we descended the steps of City Hall. A full moon was shining on a silvery bay, the delicate ironwork of the bridge made it appear as though swung in pale blue space. It was impossible to go to bed in the face of such beauty so we drove along the shore and drank in the magic of the world by moonlight.

On the subsequent evening a dinner was given in our honor by the Governor and his staff. The dining table was strewn with flowers — not one of which we had ever seen before! In this distant land are flowers and animals of prehistoric origin that exist nowhere else. After the speeches, each one was asked to describe an incident related to happiness. When it came my turn, I told a story of the Portofino Library and this met with so lively a response I was urged to tell other Bahá'í stories. After this evening requests to speak poured in, and we moved from one part of the city to another speaking of the springtime of religion.

All too quickly the days flew by until the time of departure was upon us. It was Sunday and all the friends came to tea on the boat. The sun was setting in colorful rays which swept the deck scrubbed white as sand. As we sipped our tea, the friends told me of Martha Root and of Keith Ransom-Kehler and the impression they had made during their respective visits. When the anchor chains began to rattle, Mr. Dunn drew from his pocket a Bahá'í prayer book and read the prayer for departure. Mrs. Dunn added words of loving farewell. In the world of the spirit, time and space are non-existent. Faith spans the globe, creating new and higher harmonies in the heart of man. As the shore receded I thought of the great souls everywhere working in the Cause and how some of the greatest are here in this far off land of Australia.

Chapter 34

STRANGE ADVENTURES IN NEW ZEALAND

New Zealand is divided into two islands by a wide intersecting channel. The cities of Auckland and Wellington are on the North Island and that of Christ Chirch on the South. We were now ten thousand miles from the Atlantic seacoast and only a slender slice of land lay between us and the South Pole, Tasmania. At home, spring was just around the corner while here it was autumn and, in spite of the bright sunshine, a chilly wind was blowing. I had posted a letter in Honolulu to the secretary of the Auckland Assembly telling her that I hoped to be on the *Franconia* when she docked and that I would find my way to her house without delay. We were tied at the dock before dawn. As soon as it was light the stewardess put her head in the door of my cabin. "You best hurry and dress," she said, "there is a whole crowd of people on the lower deck asking for you."

"For me? Why I don't know a soul here — there must be some mistake." "They seem to know you all right and they will be up here any minute."

I flew into my clothes and flung open the door to find sixteen Bahá'ís lined up in the corridor. To greet me they must have risen before dawn! Each one repeated the Bahá'í salutation and pressed into my hands a gift of flowers or a dainty little basket of fruit. I was overcome! What a lesson in cordiality! One believer, they told me, had had a stroke but had come as far as the wharf. I looked down and saw a wheel chair with a woman wrapped in shawls sitting in the midst of bags and barrels. We hurried to join her. The friends told me of the many opportunities they had made for me to speak.

None asked if I was accustomed to speak in public. It was taken for granted that whatever would further the Cause I would do. I asked for suggestions, since they knew their audiences, but they replied that they would pray that I would be guided to say the right thing. Their sublime confidence was contagious and I began to feel alarmingly competent and equal to any emergency.

"Before I take a step," I said, "I must buy a shoe lace. I will join you shortly at the club for breakfast."

I dashed into a shoe shop where a man armed with a long pole was raising an iron curtain from over a show window. He looked at me sharply and then darted behind a counter. He emerged with a copy of the morning newspaper. He pointed triumphantly to my photograph: "I know you came in on the *Franconia*, and you teach a new religion. I said to my wife when I read about it, 'I certainly would like to hear about a new religion — I am awfully sick of the one I have.' I go to sleep in church and my wife has to pinch me so I won't disgrace her. I need a new outlook on the heavenly kingdom and here you come to tell the very thing!"

"Well, since it's early why don't we sit down and talk it over?" I said.

"Fine! Fine! But wait, in the leather factory upstairs, there are a lot of men that would like to hear about it too."

He opened a door in the rear of the shop and called out: "I say Joe, bring the men down, there is someone here I want them to meet."

Presently the whir and spin of the machinery slowed and faded out and down the stairs came a troop of men in leather aprons reaching from the neck to the knees. They piled into the store. The shoeman, a born actor, who would have graced any stage, held aloft the newspaper displaying a row of photographs and pointing to mine said: "I want you all to hear about a new religion."

At this point, his explanation was interrupted by two customers who stepped across the threshold. "This way ladies."

He motioned them to a small sofa against the wall. "Sit there and don't stir." Hesitatingly the women advanced to the sofa and sat on the edge, alarm stamped upon their faces. Deciding that no further interruption should occur, he turned the key in the front door and dropped it in his pocket. He did not bother with my name but proceeded, in his own way, to introduce me, with many gestures, and springing lightly from one foot to the other: "This little lady that you see before you has come thousands of miles across the sea to tell us about a new religion that has sprung up in the world because there has been a new Prophet, of whom to date we know nothing. Now, if a great event like this has transpired, we ought to know about it and I am giving you this opportunity and I hope (looking severely at the customers) you will appreciate and profit by it."

I opened a little book I had in my bag and read:

> "The advent of the prophets and the revelation of the Holy Books is intended to create love between souls and friendship between the inhabitants of the earth."

I packed the Message into the fifteen minutes at my disposal. Never have I seen so rapt an audience — never has there been a more attentive one. When I finished, they remained motionless as though they had flown miles away to a higher sphere. I shook hands with each of the men telling them how interested the American Bahá'ís would be to hear of our early morning meeting. The customers, clinging together like a pair of limpets, sidled toward the door and freedom. One could imagine the story they would tell of their adventure — "We were locked in a shoe shop and someone from overseas was telling something — we could not understand what." Meanwhile the shoeman and I embraced as though we were lifelong friends and were separating for the first time. He came to all my public meetings, bringing his wife and friends, and we corresponded for years.

When I arrived at the clubhouse the friends were pacing uneasily up and down the veranda. "Where have you been?"

they asked. "When you hear of my episode, you will understand. Jacob, at least, had a ladder to mount to heaven while I had only a shoe string!"

A Woman's Rights meeting was scheduled at the club and the friends in their zeal for spreading the Bahá'í principles, had suggested that I add a word. Imagine the horror that filled the breasts of these gentle believers when the first speaker arose and with clenched fists pounded the table in front of her in an effort to arouse her sisters to a frenzy of hate as she repeated over and over such phrases as "Down with the men! They have had their way long enough! We must free the country from their claws! We must be the rulers and they the slaves." With the end of this acid tirade, the chairman turned to me and asked if I would say a word about the politics in America. I stated at once that I was a teacher and not qualified to speak on politics, but the women of America were on the whole devoted to their men and perhaps a bit lazy and glad to have them do some of the work. But since I was here I would tell a few stories in the interest of fellowship. A round of applause announced that fellowship was still popular. When I sat down someone asked if I could continue since they seldom had a chance to hear of affairs in America. The chairman, with great dignity, replied that the meeting must proceed and the delegates be heard from and that, afterwards, they would be glad to have me speak again. The backbone of hate was broken. The talks that followed were neither hot nor cold, nor did any constructive idea eventuate. Somehow the affair bogged down and I found myself again on the platform. I branched into the Bahá'í principles with special reference to the equality of men and women and how the human family was compared by 'Abdu'l-Bahá to a bird that cannot fly if there is but one wing. It must have both wings to maintain balance and to enable it to soar high above the ground. I told a few more stories to illustrate the high points of equality. We had begun the morning as a political storm center, but all such thoughts were left behind us as we advanced in the atmosphere of Bahá'í thought. Such were the confirmations of a single morning. Through the strength of prayer and the confidence and humility of the believers they had wrought a miracle!

All our evenings were devoted to public meetings. Only occasionally did we allow ourselves the privilege of spending an hour alone, where we could discuss the thrilling events in progress — the forming of the National Spiritual Assembly for Australia and New Zealand and the building of the Temple at home. My husband asked the Captain of the *Franconia* to let us give a party on board and we told him that the Maoris would come and sing and dance for us. The Captain shook his head: "I have been in and out of this harbor for twenty years. Often someone promises that the Maoris will come, but they never do. Always there is an excuse, a polite note or something comes to tell us they will not be with us."

"But, Captain," I said, "These Maoris are Bahá'ís. When they give their word, they will keep it. You will see."

That night nearly a hundred people filled the ballroom and the Maoris came, their dark beauty set off by bright shawls and beribboned skirts. They brought a noted Maori singer that we might hear their legends sung. The dancers held poi balls made of delicate tinted straw attached to their wrists. As the song proceeds, the ball is thrown in graceful circles. When the theme is sad, the ball moves slowly, if gay, faster. I could not help thinking that the ball resembled a humming bird in its motions and may have been copied from that source. The Captain, his eyes as big as saucers, stood in the doorway, unable to believe what he saw. The famous dancers of the Maoris were turning and twisting with unbelievable grace. There is something rhythmical that enters the atmosphere where different races meet together in harmony. No one present that night will, I am sure, ever forget it. Reality comes on wings of the spirit. When it is present, it sifts out sadness and care and you dwell in the secret garden of happiness.

Wellington is a night's journey by water from Auckland. We sailed along the coast whose rounded hills gave way to grim headlands. At dawn, a thin vista of water was seen running between high bluffs. The stream wound in and out until, at last, it opened like a fan into a wide bay. Here the wind is always blowing, and, to protect their gardens, high stone walls enclose the houses, and fir branches are spread along the tops of the enclosures.

There were four believers in Wellington, a brother and sister from England and a Scotchman and his wife. They had arranged a meeting at a club called "The Lyceum." But first I must take the famous drive of which they are justly proud. Reaching a hilltop, you look down on countless little villages that fringe the sea. There are whole colonies of Norwegians speaking no tongue but their own. Here also, are the quicksands with shifting layers of sand that engulf and swallow whatever touches them. Warnings are posted along the lovely looking beach to keep the unwary away. When you look upon this glistening beach and realize its terrors, it makes you conscious that in every kingdom there are pitfalls. We went back to the club. It was tastefully arranged with gay patterned curtains, a piano, and lots of books. I spoke on tradition and bade them take off their ancestral spectacles that induced near-sightedness. Bahá'u'lláh tells us in *The Seven Valleys*:

> "When the gaze of the traveler is restricted to a limited place, that is — when he looks through glasses of different colors he sees yellow, red, or white. It is due to such a view of things that conflict is stirred up among the servants, and a gloomy dust, rising from men of limitation, has enveloped the world."

Of the twenty people present, fifteen stayed and accompanied us back to the *Franconia* that was to sail in the late afternoon. My heart went out to these brave souls, strong in Faith but limited in their endeavors by the traditional thinking of the people around them. So soon the day was over! So soon the ship was winding down the ribbon of water headed for the open sea!

Chapter 35

BAHÁ'Í CLASS ON THE HIGH SEAS

If you cross the Pacific Ocean, eventually you come to the 180 Meridian. Time on our planet is set from this imaginary line. It is known as "The Date Line" and though it does not upset the ocean it does play havoc with the calendar. Let us say you arrive at the Meridian on a Wednesday, and you are travelling east! Your Wednesday will turn into Tuesday. But if you are headed towards America, your Wednesday will leap forward and become Thursday. No matter what day you start with it will be rudely snatched away and another day handed to you that you did not ask for and did not especially want. This Alice-in-Wonderland shift gave me a turn every time I crossed the Date Line. It did not, however, interfere with the Bahá'í class that I taught for three consecutive months at sea. Regularly twice a week there appeared on the bulletin board this notice:

"Bahá'í Class this afternoon, in Parlor C, 4 P. M."

The anxieties and perplexities of everyday living are stripped away at sea. People are glad to listen, more open to new ideas and not so shy. For years I heard repercussions from this class in every part of the country. For example, one day I was walking along a street in St. Paul, where I knew no one, when a woman rushed up to me and holding my arm said, "Oh, I am glad to meet you again, for though you won't believe it, I have been telling my friends about the Bahá'í Faith — and to save my life I cannot remember the name of the Interpreter — the one who came to America." "You mean 'Abdu'l-Bahá?" I asked. "Yes, yes of course! 'Abdu'l-Bahá! How

141

stupid I am to forget that title — thanks — thanks a lot!" And
she rushed on.

One morning, the Bahá'í class had two new recruits. Both
confided the special reason that had induced them to join.
"When I was a child my parents came to the United States
on a visit. It was 1912, and we were on the *Cedric* with
'Abdu'l-Bahá and his Persian suite. My family were deeply
impressed by 'Abdu'l-Bahá's appearance, though no word
passed between them. But, one day when I was alone on
deck, I passed close to the chair in which the Master was
sitting with his eyes closed. As I came near, he opened his
eyes and looked directly into mine. That glance — that never-
to-be-forgotten glance — burned into my soul. Every layer
of my being was exposed to his scrutiny. If he does not
approve a little bit of me, I thought, I shall die. At that
moment, a kindly smile lighted his face and released me from
terror. Sobs choked me, tears coursed down my cheeks, and
it was thus that my family found me. Nor was I able to explain
what had happened. In all these years, it was the one moment
of reality — always fresh in my mind. But I had not connected
you with 'Abdu'l-Bahá until this morning. Now I want to study
and understand his teachings. How strange, that again I
should be on the ocean when news of this revelation comes
towards me."

I asked if the personality of the Master impressed the
passengers. "Oh yes, everyone remarked about his majestic
bearing, his kingly walk, and above all the strange white light
that followed him everywhere."

As we turned south and the breezes freshened, another
passenger came to ask if she could join the class this afternoon.
"I want to come," she said, "because of an unusual dream I
had last night. I dreamed that I was on a highway with many
intersecting roads and I became confused as to where I was
going. I got out and walked towards a large sign at one of
the crossroads. I looked up and saw that a line had been
drawn through the directions and underneath in bold type

was written, 'This is a new cycle of human power — this is a new path, take it for it leads to the kingdom you are seeking.' This morning I opened the little blue pamphlet that lies on the library table and read: 'This is a new cycle of human power.'"

Of special interest in the class was a young American girl married to a Chinese gentleman. Their union had been bitterly opposed both by Occidental and Oriental affiliations. Reading in our pamphlets that, "Man is in the image of God, that color or race is of no importance," they had joined.

The class drew social workers, professional men and women, old and young. After each lesson we had open discussion. One afternoon a woman who had attended the lessons but had never entered into the discussions addressed the class: "I am a student of the occult and I came to learn what the Bahá'í teaching had to say about this all-important subject. Frankly, I have been disappointed since the lessons ignored this theme. The masters of the East take one to the heights! In India and Tibet are men who so control their breath that they can be buried alive without harm. They can fly through the air and walk on the water. Such achievements indicate a high spiritual degree of attainment. Is not this above the teachings you have been giving?"

"This subject is of interest to us all," I replied, "though you may again be disappointed that I do not agree with you. 'Abdu'l-Bahá assures us that from the clash of opinions comes truth. Bahá'u'lláh has given us a social program, a New World Order to bring about a higher degree of civilization. Lying underground for days means precious hours lost; nor is there any special benefit accruing to mankind from such phenomenon. 'Abdu'l-Bahá writes: 'To tamper with psychic forces while in this world interferes with the condition of the soul in the world to come. These forces are real but are not meant to be active on this plane.' Let us suppose that the captain of this ship, instead of being at the helm while we pass the dangers of the Great Barrier Reef, was out walking on the Tasman sea.

How would we feel? Would not fear of disaster choke all other sensations? But within our world there lies a spiritual world that has nothing to do with psychic phenomenon, but is connected with the spirit. It belongs to the alchemy of the spirit. Realization of the spiritual self in ourselves means realization of the exalted truth that we are from God and to Him we shall return. This return to God is the glorious goal of the Bahá'ís."

Chapter 36

I MEET THE CANNIBALS OF NEW GUINEA

All the way across the Pacific I carried a letter to an isolated Bahá'í living in Port Moresby. The Port had no harbor and we were rowed ashore in tippy little canoes. I did feel sorry for Mrs. Smith stationed on this lonely strand! I wandered up and down the street of shops asking for Mrs. Smith's whereabouts and was directed by the draper to a nearby hill crowned by a row of white houses. The direct rays of the sun on the windowpanes gave the effect of houses in perpetual motion. It did not look far, but the thermometer registered 98° and the air was laden with tropical moisture. I had not gone far before my knees gave way and I was forced to sit down. There was a comfortable looking rock by the wayside but when I put my hand on it, it was red hot like a stove, so I sat on the ground in an effort to steady my equilibrium. Presently an English soldier came over the brow of the hill followed by seven natives. Within a few paces of me, they flung themselves down and the young commander took off his topee and began fanning himself.

"Cruising?" he remarked, glancing out to where the *Franconia* lay at anchor. I nodded, "But I had not reckoned with such heat as this." "Don't I know," he exclaimed, "haven't we just done three miles of it." "Do you have to walk? Is there no other way to get around the Island?" "Usually we fly — no roads you know in the interior — a few ponies around the Port — but they're useless in the jungle. You could not take a plane where I have been — I had to walk it. We saw smoke from the tribal ovens early this morning and had already heard that a fight was in progress. We knew what to expect."

145

The sudden knowledge of the dreadful crime stopped my heart beat: "CANNIBALS?" I whispered under my breath. He nodded. "They are not a bad lot really — did not give me a bit of trouble, put out the fires and came right along. They know that the British government won't stand for these heathen practices. But here's the hitch — it's part of their religion. As far back as the tribes can reckon, the conquered enemy has been devoured. The belief that qualities are transferred — that bravery enters into the tribe by consuming the conquered; but we have to compromise and make the punishment light. Christianity seemed to confuse them even more, for they find in communion a pattern like that of their own belief and in the crucifixion a saving grace through the shedding of blood. So we don't know just how to handle it — we just lock them up and let it go at that!"

Superstition! How slow we are to cure it! Bahá'u'lláh placed science beside religion to give us a twofold weapon to fight it. But are we of the civilized world free of it? I remembered that the apartment houses of New York omit the number 13 and skip from 12 to 14, fearing that people would believe it unlucky to live on the thirteenth floor. Pedestrians step out into the road to avoid walking under a ladder, we knock on wood, cross our fingers and give evidence of our belief in signs and numbers the world over!

My meditations were interrupted by the natives scrambling to their feet. Suddenly I remembered the errand on which I had set out and appealed to the soldier for the whereabouts of Mrs. Smith. He shook his head, "I don't know the womenfolk, but the jailer will. He knows everybody and he can tell you about them all — he's our newspaper."

I joined the procession. First came the lieutenant, then the natives shuffling their feet in the heavy dust and I brought up the rear. The jail was only a pink frame house with bent bars at the windows and the jailer, a Mr. James by name, fingered the envelope I handed him and looking up with a bright knowing air, remarked: "Ah, Mrs. Smith — she's a fine lady, but she is not here right now. She boarded *The Empress* last Monday on the steamer's way to Sydney to buy clothes for her three children. I declare those children grow out of their suits while you're buttoning them up."

The prisoners crowded in and looked from one single window, they nodded to me shyly and, as I passed, one man dropped a wilted flower into my hand. Had it adorned the brow of a warrior as he hurried forth to battle in the pale dawn — who can say?

As I turned to retrace my steps, Mr. James called to me. "As your co-religionist is not here, why don't you come with me and see a native Christening? It's worth seeing once, and I'll tell Mrs. Smith that I entertained you in her absence."

Panting and perspiring I hurried along trying to keep pace with him. We were soon at the shore where the native houses are built on stiles over the water. We mounted a rickety flight of steps into a room with no doors and with floor boards so far apart that you were forced to leap from one to the other, while dark water rushed underneath. There was no furniture in the room. A government official was standing on one of the boards and the father of the baby on another. Hanging on the wall, wrapped in something or other, was the baby, and a pig in a wicker basket rested uneasily on a rough stone hearth. No sound came from the infant, but the pig cried softly while the father addressed him: "Oh pig, we are sending you to the river gods and to the forest gods and we want you to tell them that we are poor people. We cannot send them fine gifts like our neighbors because the fishing is poor and the land is poor and we haven't enough to eat. You won't forget to tell them that — will you pig? It is important that they should know and help us."

The pig, I fear, was more concerned with his immediate future than with messages to distant gods and now began to squeal loudly. The father seized the basket, and, with a long knife in his teeth, hurried down the steps. The sounds of protest from the pig were horrible, but at length silence fell and the father, bearing the pig's liver on a board, returned. Over the liver the government official, the jailer and the father bent their heads. Divination by means of a liver was a subtile and complicated affair. The father, a born pessimist, seemed to find no cheering news written upon the scroll of life as represented by the liver. But the official, whose duty it was to find something encouraging, pointed to a white thread: "That augers well," he remarked. Mr. James, always dramatic, now took over. He straightened up, spread out his hands and in a voice as though reciting "The boy stood on the burning deck" exclaimed: "The boy will go to sea — he will go to sea!" At these words, the father crumpled up with a bitter glance at the jailer and said: "And what else could he do, I want to know." Mr. James, who evidently had anticipated this remark, now hurled his bomb: "I don't see fishing as a livelihood in this liver. What I see is service — service in His Majesty's navy no less — here are the marks — the marks of a career to be proud of."

I could see that the father was not wholly convinced of the grand future of his son, but he could not argue with a superior and so left it at that. The official seemed greatly relieved to hear that the future was settled and promptly took his leave. As we withdrew I could see the mother's eye glued to one of the cracks in the wall. We moved gingerly down the steps and when out of earshot, the official wiped his brow, "I don't know one thing about all this business and if you hadn't come along, Mr. James, I think I would have found that long knife between my ribs."

Mr. James received this news with consummate pride. "I just go along with their old-time customs," he said, "and tell them what they want to hear like any right minded fortune teller." So saying, we parted, and I walked down the long rickety wharf with these soul stirring adventures locked in my breast.

Chapter 37

ONE MORNING IN MANILA

It was early spring when the *Franconia* drew into the Bay
of Manila. Before the Japanese invasion the city appeared as
though made of spun sugar — everything was white, lacy, and
as impermanent as a city in a dream. We had been promised
twelve hours ashore — time was needed to place the Spanish
pamphlets to the best advantage. Alas, when the gangplank
was in place the bulletin board announced we were sailing at
noon, because of tides and wind and matters that admitted
of no argument.

We rushed down to the wharf, dived into a carriage and
asked the driver to take us to a book store — the biggest and
best in town. He nodded and set off at a brisk pace, and drew
up before a large and imposing shop. We explained to the
man behind the counter the purpose of our visit. "No," he
said, shaking his head vigorously, "no book could be accepted
or sold here without the stamp of the Archbishop of Manila.
We must go at once and have him stamp it." But I said meek-
ly, "It is not a Catholic book." He looked horrified — never
would such a book be put on his shelves or for that matter on
the shelves of any shop in the city! His words proved only
too true — everywhere we turned the reply was the same —
unless stamped by the Archbishop. Two hours wasted —
golden drops of time falling into space — what would we do?
Was there a college in Manila? Yes, and the driver whipped
up the pony and we drove to the President's house. Our reception was courteous. If the literature was anti-Catholic, said
the President, they did not want it. "Oh no," I replied, "it's

149

not anti-anything but dedicated to universal principles that would relate all religions and bring them closer together. After considerable thought he said, "In the college we have a small shelf allotted to comparative religions — it is overcrowded now but you might try — the librarian is a very liberal minded man." We thanked him and hurried on, scarcely daring to look at the time. Frantic anxiety must have showed in my face as I broached the request to the librarian to accept a few pamphlets for the shelf of comparative religions. I held up the thinnest one to let him see how little space it would require. "Very well," he replied thoughtfully, "I will take one into the other room and look it over, perhaps we could keep one." Up and down the narrow room I paced, praying fervently, beseeching Bahá'u'lláh to soften the heart of this man and permit these precious words to remain on the Island. In a short time the librarian returned smiling and said, "There is nothing adverse in your little book. You may place one or two of the Spanish pamphlets on that top shelf." I hurried forward and pushed the thick volumes apart with all my strength, and left four small volumes shining out from among the ancient faiths that stood on either side.

Just as the gong sounded for the last fifteen minutes before sailing, we mounted the gangplank. So far to come, so little accomplished, rang the sad refrain in my heart. But this is God's Cause and it is HE, and not we, who brings forth the blossoms and the fruit!

When the *Franconia* docked in San Francisco in April, 1938, a letter awaited me, postmarked from the Philippines, and signed, "Maddela." It read: "Only a few days after your visit to Manila, I left Solano and went on a business trip to Manila, where, having time to spare, I dropped into the reading room at the college library. On the shelf of comparative religions I found four new books. I took one down and sat enthralled. This was the religion I had been seeking! One after another I read the four booklets, forgetting time and place. Finally I took my pencil and jotted down sentence after sentence. Then, as in a dream, I returned to Solano; called my wife and our families and told them that the religion we had so earnestly sought was the Bahá'í Faith and that we must all embrace it."

Before long the Bahá'í community had grown to fifty members. When war broke out all communication ceased with the Maddelas or with the Bahá'í Assembly of Solano. The weary months dragged on until the summer of 1945. Then, in September, once again news winged its way from the Philippines — this time from the devoted Bahá'í, Alvin Blum, attached to a medical unit with the United States Army.

"I left the 249th General Hospital in Manila," wrote Sgt. Blum, "where I am stationed and hitch-hiked 223 miles to reach Solano to find your Bahá'í Assembly. Solano is in ruins. It had been a thriving city of more than twenty thousand people before the war, while now it is reduced to only a few thousand. I soon located the Maddelas, happy and full of spirit in spite of their impoverished condition. Before the war they had been influential and well established but when the Japanese came they were forced to leave everything and flee for their lives. Now, with ten people living together, they have only a grass hut of one room. They cook over an open fireplace and their dishes and cooking utensils are crude and handmade. Of the fifty enrolled Bahá'ís twenty-five have been killed or are missing. For three years the Maddelas hid in rice fields, living under such conditions that it was miraculous they survived. As a result of the bombings and terrible hardships, Mr. Maddela's hair turned white and he became totally deaf. They were all overjoyed to see a Bahá'í, their first visitor, and we talked of our beloved Faith until night fell and I went to a nearby hospital to sleep. There I secured food and clothing for them and we had another happy reunion in the morning. They are fine intelligent people; both Mr. and Mrs. Maddela have taught school. Before the war they had built with great effort, a Bahá'í Center, and had placed a sign at the entrance inviting everyone to come to their Bahá'í reading room. At last, they told me, when they were able to come out from their hiding places in the rice fields, they returned to find the city a mass of rubble, their home destroyed. Only one thing was standing! It was a sign which read:

'BAHÁ'Í CENTER — READING ROOM
EVERYBODY WELCOME' "

Chapter 38

THE PHILANTHROPIC PIG

The Dollar Line dropped us off at Honolulu on our way home from the East. Oh, the bliss of seeing familiar shapes and contours. Oh, the joy of standing on ground hallowed by association. How homelike everything looked after the panorama of strange scenes and places. The Bahá'ís were happy too, and we spent much time together. So much to hear — so much to say — there seemed no end to our conversation! One evening one of the Bahá'ís, a nurse, drew me aside: "I am sad tonight," she said, "my heart is heavy; for a great wrong has been done to one of my patients. He is a poor man with cancer of the face and the disease prevents him from working. But he has been able to earn sufficient for his needs by raising pigs. Last night, wicked men drove to the pen and stole Mother Maisie, who was just about to have a family and make Noel happy. This morning we found the pen empty!"

"Goodness me," I exclaimed, "there must be more than one pig on the Island. Why don't we buy another?" In the triumph of home-coming a mere pig presented no hazard at all!

My Bahá'í friend sighed, "No use looking for that one. She is undoubtedly slaughtered by now."

"Well, not that identical pig," I cried, "but one just as good." "Do you believe you could find one?" she remarked doubtfully.

"Do I think I can buy a pig? Certainly I do. What on earth is going to prevent me?"

"I don't know," she answered sadly, "I understand it is

153

complicated and difficult — but if you think you could it would be an act of real charity."

"Leave it to me," I cried gaily, an ecstasy of satisfaction oozing from every pore. "Leave it to me."

"Very well," she said, and was going on to give me reasons for her doubts but thought better of it and merely smiled and walked away.

Slowly, the facts concerning the sale of livestock were assembled. The market was at Pearl Harbor, twenty miles distant from the Hotel Halekulani, where we stayed. The time of animal selling was 3 a. m. Frantically I searched for a man who owned a cart and who would be willing to drive in the middle of the night. The hotel employees shook their respective heads. They knew no one that crazy! But, at the eleventh hour, I found a friend-in-need in the person of a Chinese laundry boy. He had a cousin and that cousin had a horse and cart and was no stranger to early hours. A bargain was struck. My guide was part Chinese, part Hawaiian, and had a dash of Malay and indeed, he had the prowess of all three races. He knew short-cuts hidden from the eyes of the haughty motorists and his tired looking horse maintained a surprising gait. Jogging over by-roads and no-roads, we appeared over the crest of the hill as the Navy-yard clock was striking three. It was bedlam. Squeals and squeaks rent the air, horses neighed, cocks crowed — cows mooed, singly and in battalions. You could hardly make yourself heard. Men with flares and much-spotted white aprons were banging doors of pens and calling to each other. I was unprepared for this seething mass of animal life and greatly subdued, I asked timidly, "What shall I ask for?"

"Ask for one about to bear an immediate pig," he answered.

I walked down the aisle between the pens until I came to the fattest animal on record, her sides bulged and seemed to flow and fill all space. I pulled a man's sleeve. In the half light, he seemed to have a certain resemblance to the creature on the ground. "Is this an immediate pig?" I ventured.

"Sure! Lucky if you get home."

My guide was right at my elbow to seal the bargain and added quickly, "I'll back up the cart and get help."

The operation was by no means simple. To while away the time, I bought a roll of mosquito netting and festooned the pig, tying big white bows around her portly middle, a double fluffy one on the curly tail and bowknots round the ears. When the monster was securely tied in the cart, we set off. I reflected that the nurse had reasons for her doubts — thread was all the enterprise hung by! We arrived at the empty pen and my driver proudly produced a plank with which, with great presence of mind, he had provided himself. The board was fastened to the end of the cart and the pig was induced, by fair means or foul, to move forward until she could be pushed into the pen.

I was exhausted; so was the driver. As for the horse his feet dragged — his head brushed the ground. I believe we were all three asleep on that drive.

Late in the afternoon I called the nurse suggesting that we drive out and see how things at the farm were going. It was a lovely day with now and again liquid sunshine, as the short showers are called. As we approached a field near the farm, we saw people kneeling on the grass. The nurse, recognizing several in the crowd, called out, "What is this? What has happened?"

"Have you not heard — why there has been a miracle! It is the feast of St. Ann and she answered Noel's prayer and sent him a pig — if you don't believe it look in the pen, there are bits of white clouds still hanging on the creature!"

Who were we to disturb the devout? Silently we clambered into the motor and quietly backed away from the scene. We looked at each other. "Yes," we said, "We too, believe in miracles!"

Part Six
South Africa

Chapter 39

HORIZONS WIDENED

Africa! We were to have ten days in this unknown land before sailing through the Indian Ocean for the East. And ten glorious days they were. Field Marshal Jan Smuts was Prime Minister and it was necessary to ask permission to speak in public before putting a foot on a platform. I sent a note saying I was a Bahá'í and that I wished to speak about it. In his reply he mentioned that he admired greatly the Bahá'í principles but that religion was such a controversial matter that he hoped I would choose another theme. As in South America where I had been forced to open a campaign by talking on the theater, so now an idea popped into my mind of how I could satisfy the law and at the same time give the Message. But to go back a little. My husband had letters of introduction to Mr. and Mrs. Askerland and they had arranged a public meeting for me at a handsome club and had invited the elite of Capetown to be present. The Prime Minister had sent flowers and was represented by a high titled dignitary. There was to be a supper. Dressed in my best I mounted the platform and announced that after a short talk on the miracle of Frozen Foods (a commodity that had just come upon the markets of America) I would join each group during the supper and speak of something vital, inspiring and impossible to give from a public stand at the present time. The method worked beyond my wildest dreams. They were to hear something special — something like a secret and as I sat down at each table they gave me their undivided attention. They questioned

159

me — they expressed the interest that every teacher longs to arouse. The meeting was distinctly Bahá'í after all.

We visited Victoria Falls, a sight my husband had much desired to see. One mile of falling water! It not only fell but roared and foamed and covered the forest with spray. A puny dot on the landscape was a human being beside a power like that of creation itself. I was glad to leave it though thrilled by the opportunity to view its mighty force. Next we entered Kruger National Park, one of the great wild animal reservations of the world. Fortunately the smell of gasoline is hateful in their nostrils and one may drive, if windows are closed, with perfect impunity among them. A parade of lions stretched across the road and forced our car to the edge of the ditch, but not a muscle moved and not an ear twitched among the kings of the forest. The tigers are nervous and only their yellow eyes peer out from the bushes as a car passes by.

I was to speak at Bulawayo to the teachers and ministers who had invited me to do so. My train was four hours late and the rain was pelting down in rivers. My audience had waited, however, and received my talk with warmth and real interest. It was a meeting I shall never forget. When I finished, I asked if there was anyone who would distribute the Bahá'í pamphlets for me, since we were sailing next day. A slender man held up his hand, the Rabbi of Bulawayo. Until his death, five years later, we corresponded and he spread over his part of the country more than seven hundred Bahá'í pamphlets. This unique city has the widest streets in the world, since they were laid out to turn eighteen and twenty yoke of oxen.

High up among the boulders is the tomb of Cecil Rhodes, a site that suggests the rugged beginnings of civilization. It is a city with progressive education and lovely people.

We embarked at Durban. Leaning from the rail of the *Franconia*, we watched the Zulu giants load the ship. On their coal black wiry hair war bonnets were perched, their long slender legs were whitened; their feet had natural pads that makes them spring into the air with every step — step is not the right word to use, for they bound as naturally as we move close to the earth when we walk. Goodbye Africa! Some day I am coming back.

Chapter 40

OUR INGENUITY CHALLENGED

In a letter from the Guardian in 1948 he indicated that it would be useful to have me go to South Africa. I jumped at the chance. "Go," wrote the beloved, "not later than August and take Ophelia Crum with you."

Keenly we searched the listings of the steamship lines. No ships seemed to be headed for South Africa except the Robbin Line, but soon we learned that ladies unaccompanied by a male were taboo. Tucked away in a sailing prospectus we found a freighter sailing from New Orleans, that carried twelve passengers (sex not mentioned) and we booked space immediately. At this time Marion Little was living in New Orleans and we hurried down south and fitted ourselves into her cozy little house. All unknown to us, our dear friend Marcia Steward had left Chili where she has been pioneering and had flown to Miami bound for California via New Orleans. Here she had a four-hour wait for the California train and picking up a morning paper she learned that we were in the city, prior to sailing for South Africa and that we were guests of Mrs. Little. To our intense surprise we saw Marcia alight at Marion's door. Blown from divers directions we huddled together and discussed our future plans — Marion preparing to leave for Europe — Marcia to Honduras and we to South Africa. No sooner had Marcia torn herself away to catch her train than the Lykes Line telephoned that they were sailing that night. We knew that mere passengers were incidental — when the cargo was on board the ship sailed.

It was raining hard when we embarked on the *Mason*

Lykes. It was a pleasant surprise to find our cabin roomy and comfortable. Freighters carry no stewards — when a seaman has made your bed that is the extent of the ship's obligation to its passengers. If the sea is running high and one cannot navigate the winding stairs to the dining room, one is forced to fast. If ill, there is no doctor, no nurse, no medicine. We missed none of these — for we proved to be perfect sailors. The voyage starts with a twelve-hour run down the Mississippi. During the passage across the Gulf of Mexico the Captain changed our course three times to avoid the path of hurricanes. Day followed day upon an empty ocean — not a craft did we encounter — not a sail lightened the horizon — not even a fish rose from the deep to greet us. Lulled by the monotony of motion we read and crocheted, I comparing stitches with the Captain, a great hand with the needle and proud of his embroidery. At the end of twenty-one days the lights of Capetown stretched across the green waters and came shimmering through the falling rain. Land! Solid earth! What a miracle to see again a tree rising above us. Capetown is scenic in the highest degree, flanked by the Atlantic on the west, the Indian ocean on the east, with the waters of the Antarctic stretching far to the south; locked from the rest of the continent by a long level mountain named Table, whose top is often covered by feathery clouds that fall over its ridge, giving an appearance of an embroidered table cloth. As one looks up it seems the perfect design of a table set for the gods and peopled by fabled giants of mythology.

Beneath a wealth of beauty are many problems hard to understand. The major one is the status of the colored people. Long ago their forebears were slaves brought down from upper Africa to serve, but many strains of blood and many generations have since then produced the present race of intelligent, industrious people. They are as different from the natives (those who have recently come from the bush) as they are from the Dutch or English; nevertheless they are classed with the native and banned by an act of segregation that is unjust.

Because the native must live outside the city limits, so must they. "Apartheid," meaning segregation, is rampant under the present government. Speaking of the Negro quarters of Cape-town, the historian, Henry Gibbs, writes in *Twilight in South Africa:* "Beyond Roeland Street and the old castle lying behind the railroad station is a narrow, slightly looping street. It is named Canterbury. In Britain Canterbury means Christianity for the English people. In Capetown it means slums." Here you will find houses of despair, as a reporter from the Cape Argus newspaper aptly calls them.

But all this was hidden from us the night of our arrival. On the dock under a huge umbrella stood Mr. Scott of the South African Travel Bureau who greeted us as soon as the gangplank was in place. He dashed with us through the rain to the shelter of the Arthur's Seat Hotel. We sat in our narrow bedroom planning our teaching campaign. First Johannesburg, the largest city, then Pretoria, Durban, and last Capetown, since it would be our port of departure. The next day we took the famous Blue Train that winds from the mountains near the coast, over the veldt, through Kimberly to Johannesburg. We settled at the new Skyline Hotel and after prayerful consultation decided to place in the Johannesburg Star, an invitation reading:

> "People of good will are needed to step forward and join a class now being formed, based on the following Principles: Independent investigation of truth; The Foundation of all Religions is one; Religion must be in accord with science and reason; We must work together for Universal Peace, beginning with the individual."

From this first publicity we received thirty-three letters and to each we sent a Bahá'í pamphlet so that they would be apprised of the basis of our teaching. From this second appeal came fifteen acceptances and on a Monday night we opened the doors for our class. Unknowingly we had stumbled on a holiday and only two men appeared, an optimist and a pessimist, but both stuck with us to the end of our stay. In a recent letter from the pessimist he wrote that he had told God that Loulie Mathews was to do his praying for him. Many women could not come in the evening and asked for a morning meeting. In a few weeks we had sixteen regular pupils in this class. Among the group was a Mrs. J. D. Rheinalt Jones, whose husband was the Representative of the primary native schools, the only education accorded by the government. Through Mrs. Jones' influence I was able to speak at all the native schools, including two privately run institutions, one Catholic and one Jewish. Our search for a taxi driver without prejudice took the cooperation of the waiters and porters of the hotel. Finally a sympathetic friend appeared and off we went and visited nine schools in succession. The driver accompanied us into the schools and often added weight to the platform while I was speaking. The children are taught in "African," a simplified Dutch. This language is gradually superseding English in South Africa and is forced upon the people by the present administration.

We crowned our opportunities among the native schools by meeting Rev. Ray E. Phillips and his wife. Thirty years ago they had come from the United States as missionaries to South Africa. Destiny ordered that they cross the path of Mr. Jan H. Hofmeyer, a philanthropist with a dream under his hat. His dream was to establish a center for the natives who were pouring into Johannesburg. Finding the Phillipses an ideal couple for the accomplishment of his ideas, he built in solid stone a home, a library and a compound for these bewildered children of nature. Ophelia and I spent a Sunday evening with them in their recreation hall. I spoke on the Bahá'í principles and they told me of their experiences in a white world. One young man described his difficulties in seeking a position as teacher. He had been trained at Lovedale but found the schoolhouse doors closed against him. In desperation he gathered the children of the village where he lived and taught them reading and writing by the roadside. This pied piper of education drew around him the children from far and wide; consternation spread among those in authority until they were forced to offer a roof beneath which to hold his classes. We were reminded of Alan Paton's words in *Cry, the Beloved Country* — "We believe in the brotherhood of man but not for South Africa — we believe in help for the underdog, but here we want him to stay under. The truth is that our civilization is riddled through and through with dilemma . . . Our civilization is a tragic compound of great ideal and fearful practice, of high assurance and desperate anxiety, of loving charity and fearful clutching of possessions."

In the midst of Bahá'í activities a note arrived that said: "I am sending a motor for you and Miss Crum to come for lunch. You do not know me under my present name but we are old friends as you will see." Much intrigued by this new adventure we set off. As the car drew up to the house, we saw indeed, standing on the doorstep, an old friend, Cornelia Moody. She is the daughter of Dwight Lyman Moody, famous evangelist of the eighteen-eighties, who, with I. D. Sankey, revolutionized certain Christian services by introducing spirited and rhythmic hymns that stirred the blood and filled the churches. Cornelia, now the wife of our Consul General, Charles E. Dickerson, planned many openings for us. What a gay luncheon we had! How we enjoyed home cooking and the dainty table at which we sat. The Dickersons were in the throes of moving to Pretoria and they invited us to visit them there — an invitation we gladly accepted. When they were settled again came the motor and sped us to the door of the United States Embassy in Pretoria.

Pretoria lies on two levels. The higher dominates the city with its handsome municipal buildings. Gardens spill down the slopes with vermilion cannas peeking out from every fold of the descending hills. On the lower level the city streets are lined with the spectacular Jacaranda trees, now covered with lavendar blossoms. These trees turn the world mauve. Below them they form a secret world that shuts out the sharp blue of the sky above.

Whenever we had time from our teaching engagements, we took the list of Fanny Knobloch's former class and searched the city for them. It was discouraging, for over twenty years had passed and the people had moved away, many had died and we looked upon the white corner house — our last address — with depressed sighs. Here lived Peter Cruse, a blind music teacher who had been a member of the Bahá'í class. He still lived there and welcomed us with delight. When he heard the brilliant record of the Faith under the banner of the Guardian he was astonished. In the course of conversation he mentioned Agnes Carey who had belonged to the class and was now living in Durban. He was sure she had remained interested in the Faith.

In a few days we returned to Johannesburg. When we were free we took a plane for Durban to find Agnes Carey. Agnes who had seen no Bahá'í for twenty years and we who had sought in vain for one true believer met as though lifelong friends. We were submerged in emotion. Agnes had kept in touch with Shoghi Effendi and her inner convictions had withstood the march of time and loneliness. She had arranged a Bahá'í talk at the Theosophical rooms and many heard the Message for the first time. On Sunday we gave an informal tea and twelve who had attended the public meeting came and brought their questions, and conversation, like the tide in a creek, swept over and blotted out the hours. Since returning to America Agnes has written us of her own activities that are being richly blessed.

During our stay in Durban the American Consul, Mr. J. S. McGregor, and his wife took us up their steep hill to lunch. Their house overlooked terraces of tropical flowers and in the distance sparkled the Indian Ocean. We were overjoyed to find them both familiar with the Faith; he, because he had attended Antioch College with members of the Master's family, and she, because she had been at school with Amelie Pompelly. He told us with great pride of the recent visit of an American warship and of the excellent behavior of the men while on leave. Our parting with the McGregors was temporary as we planned to meet them later in Pretoria.

We were attracted to the handsome shops of the East Indian traders in Durban. Many years ago these people had been brought to South Africa to work in the cotton fields. The work for which they were brought was not congenial and beyond their strength and was soon abandoned. It will be remembered that Gandhi was here in 1894 and remained for more than twenty years, to help them with their problems. We walked the sunny streets gazing at the lovely materials that lined the windows. We had no foreknowledge of the tragic events that occurred some weeks later. The incident that brought about a fierce race riot was seemingly unimportant. A native boy named George had come to meet his brother in front of Bannath's store. In this merchant's employ was a slightly older boy who often had mild sparring matches with the native boy. The exact details will never be known, but, George either fell or was pushed through the plate glass window of the Bannath shop. The impact of George and the window made history. Like a flame of fire rumor spread to the Zulu settlements. One of their number had been murdered — their enemies the East Indians had shot one of their tribe. Like a cloud of black thunder the Zulus descended on Victoria Street armed with sticks and stones, with staves and knives. When the worst was over one hundred and ninety-two lay dead in the streets, more than a thousand were carried to the hospitals, street after street was burning, the handsome district round Victoria Street was a heap of rubble. Armed forces arrived from Pretoria, and aid was sought from as far away as Capetown, before the rebellion was quelled. Nor is race antagonism the only tinder box. There is religion.

The sun was shining as we flew back to Johannesburg, happy in our recent visit. The entire class greeted us and at the first meeting expressed a desire to write the Guardian a letter of appreciation of the Teachings of Bahá'u'lláh and of their intention to continue their study. We left them a set of books and a course to follow. We had already been successful in placing several Bahá'í books in the public library. After doing all we could to impress each one with their responsibility for acquiring a deeper understanding, we again entered the Blue Train, bound for the southern shore.

In Capetown we found space at the Mt. Nelson Hotel, near to the heart of the city. We bemoaned the absence of the Askelands who had furthered my Bahá'í talks during my former visit. They were away in Norway but we had counted without the rock-like quality of their friendship. Now came a letter from Norway — fat with information. They were giving a tea for us in Capetown and had invited some sixty guests to hear the Bahá'í Message. They had by letters attended to every detail and when we arrived at the club where the party was given, we found a hostess, flowers on each table, maids in dainty aprons ready to serve and all the sixty guests were there! They listened with concentrated attention as I unfolded the Divine Plan. When the talk was finished and tea and cakes were served, we had an hour of sociability and I met several who had heard me before. Though we inserted in the Cape Argus the same advertisement as in Johannesburg no answers appeared in the mail box. Christmas was approaching and a pitch of activity was apparent among the people. We were not lacking individual students however, and we made many friends for the Faith.

On Christmas Day we waved farewell to beautiful Capetown and sailed by the Castle Line for England.

Conclusion

THE NEW FRONTIER

And thus, having done my utmost to roar across the Seven Seas, I turn now with gratitude to Shoghi Effendi, our beloved Guardian, whose staunch support and sympathetic guidance has been a never failing beacon light throughout these journeys.

He has now opened a new and dramatic episode, calling into action the National Spiritual Assemblies of five countries; England, Iran, Egypt, India and America, to unite in a concerted plan to send pioneers to settle in Africa. Its importance is indicated by the Guardian's words:

> "Indeed the birth of this African enterprise, in the opening decade of the second Bahá'í Century . . . should be acclaimed as an event of peculiar significance in the evolution of our beloved Faith."

Thus the Bahá'í Message will encircle the earth.

Though the Herald Prophet was put to death by a fanatical people; Bahá'u'lláh imprisoned; the Interpreter of His Words persecuted, and thousands of martyrs stained red the soil of Persia; yet the message of hope has flown round the world. The hour is dark and perilous but thoughtful individuals are seeking solutions to the global problems. The outline for world peace and unity as enunciated in the divine Revelation of Bahá'u'lláh is permeating the consciousness of mature people everywhere. The dawn of the Golden Age is pulsating through the minds of men. Let us hasten, hasten towards the Promised Day.